STOCK CONTROL SYSTEMS AND RECORDS
Second edition

Stock Control Systems and Records

Peter Baily and Gerard Tavernier

Second Edition by
Richard Storey

Gower

in association with
the Institute of Purchasing and Supply

© Gower Publishing Company Limited 1984

All rights reserved. No part of this publication may be reproduced, stored in a retrieval system, or transmitted in any form or by any means, electronic, mechanical, photocopying, recording, or otherwise without the prior permission of Gower Publishing Company Limited.

First published 1973 by Gower Press Limited as
Design of Stock Control Systems and Records.

Second edition published 1984 by
Gower Publishing Company Limited
Aldershot, Hants, England

Printed in Great Britain by
Biddles Ltd, Guildford, Surrey

British Library Cataloguing in Publication Data

Storey, Richard
   Stock control systems and records. — 2nd ed.
   1. Inventory control
   I. Title II. Baily, Peter. Design of stock control systems and records III. Tavernier, Gerard
   658.7'87 TS160

   ISBN 0-566-02363-6

Contents

LIST OF ILLUSTRATIONS vii

PREFACE ix

ACKNOWLEDGMENTS xi

PUBLISHER'S NOTE xii

Part One ORGANISATION AND CONTROL

1 PRINCIPLES OF STOCK CONTROL 3
Need for a system—the right approach—stock control objectives—customer satisfaction—measuring performance—responsiveness to change—management reports

2 ORGANISING THE STOCK CONTROL FUNCTION 11
Stock control and other functions—materials management—production and stock control at Fords—job specification

3 APPLICATION OF BASIC CONTROL TECHNIQUES 19
Colour codes for usage classes—analysis by computer—controlling stock levels—ruled-bin system—statistical stocktaking

| 4 | DESIGN OF STOCK RECORDS | 33 |

Designing forms—filing systems

| 5 | COMPUTERS AND STOCK CONTROL | 53 |

Computer history—application of a computer to stock control—assessing the computer market—the implementation process—to separate or to integrate?—case studies—the elements of computer systems

Part Two   CASE STUDIES; SYSTEMS FOR SERVICE INDUSTRIES AND MANUFACTURING PROCESSES

| 6 | STOCK CONTROL IN SERVICE INDUSTRIES | 75 |

Greater London Council supplies department—Barnet Health Authority supplies system—Marks and Spencer

| 7 | MANUFACTURING PROCESSES | 87 |

H W Ward and Company—Colt International—Ford Motor Company Limited—Pfizer Limited

APPENDIX: CHECKLIST FOR ANALYSING EFFECTIVENESS OF STOCK CONTROL SYSTEM   123

AFTERWORD   125

INDEX   127

Illustrations

2.1	Materials management: organisation chart	15
3.1	80/20 listing (extract)	22-3
3.2	Two-bin system	25
3.3	Service level: daily analysis	26
3.4	Stock ratio analysis	29
4.1	Forms design guide, HMSO	35
4.2	Strip indexing	39
4.3	Strip index cards, Kalamazoo	40
4.4	Rotary file	41
4.5	Rotary index file cards, C W Cave	42
4.6	Stores record visible-index cards, Kalamazoo	43
4.7	Stores ledger visible-index cards, Kalamazoo	44, 45
4.8	Stock analysis visible-index card, Kalamazoo	46
4.9	Allocation visible-index card, Kalamazoo	47
4.10	Stock balance record card, Kardex	48
4.11	Visible-index card with overleaf, Kardex	48
4.12	Order and stock visible-index record card, Roneo	49
4.13	Visible-edge forms trays	50
4.14	Selecting slotted file cards from the sorter, Findex system	51
4.15	Edge-punched card	51
4.16	Prepunched form	52
5.1	'Apple' mini-computer	54
5.2	ABS mini-computer system	55
6.1	GLC stock replenishment notice	78
6.2	GLC items in arrear: weekly listing	80-1
7.1	Stock movement and levels control, H W Ward	89
7.2	Weekly reorder tabulation, H W Ward	93

7.3	Price review listing, H W Ward	93
7.4	Typical structure of product planning and control, Ford	99
7.5	Material information system, Ford	100
7.6	Release authorisation, Ford	106
7.7	Stock status report, Ford	108
7.8	Critical shortage report, Ford	112
7.9	Requisition/purchase order form, Pfizer	118
7.10	New stock item request form, Pfizer	120
7.11	Application for additions to engineering stores, Pfizer	121

Preface

Stock control is probably one of the most neglected areas of management, and international comparisons of the effective stock usage rate (stock 'turnround') show a very large gap between the best and the worst. This factor, together with the high interest rates that currently prevail, means that resources tied up in slow moving stocks are a severe drag on commercial success.

Based almost entirely on the experience and techniques of some of the most progressive organisations in the UK, this book is intended to serve as a practical aid to the design and implementation of logical procedures and systems in the stock control function.

This second edition explores the use of computers in the application of stock control and, in particular, examines the case for a small computer dedicated to stores and stock control, as distinct from the normal concept of partial (and therefore remote) use of a large system operated from the centre of the organisation.

A further addition deals with stock control approaches in the service industries, which jointly embrace a huge investment in stock in order to meet the needs of central and local government, the armed forces, the health and water industries, leisure and retail sectors, and many more in the non-manufacturing area.

It is hoped that this publication will help persuade more organisations that investment in stock warrants serious attention and that an effective and properly managed form of stock control procedure can lead to significant saving of space, equipment and cash.

Richard Storey

Acknowledgments

I am indebted to the following companies for allowing me to assess their stock control operations at length in preparing for this book:

Colt International, Havant, Hampshire
Ford Motor Company, Warley, Brentwood, Essex
Marks and Spencer, London
Pfizer, Sandwich, Kent
H W Ward and Company, Worcester

I am particularly grateful to the Barnet Health Authority and to the supplies officer there, who provided valuable assistance in describing what is probably one of the most effective health service supply operations in the country; and to the managing director of Medoc Computers Ltd., of Nottingham, for a very large contribution to the chapter on computers. My thanks must go also to the many suppliers of office records and forms, especially Kalamazoo Ltd, for providing me with useful information and advice.

R.S.

Publisher's Note

The illustrative material in this book is drawn from the actual documents used by a variety of companies, to whom acknowledgments are expressed on the previous pages.

The need for a standard format in book reproduction means that the size and proportions of many documents have had to be modified in the following pages. The essential information carried by each form, however, remains unaltered. Firms using this book to design or adapt their own stock control system will, of course, draw up forms of a shape and size to suit their own requirements, adding appropriate data covering company name, reference numbers or dates, specific instructions, etc.

Part One

ORGANISATION AND CONTROL

1

Principles of Stock Control

The fundamental principles and objectives of stock control are just the same, whether the stock to be controlled is in a small shop or a large factory. Differences of scale mask the fundamental identity. The practical applications and procedures are, of course, very diverse, from the rudimentary documentation of the small store to the tape files and elaborate computer printouts of the big systems, described later.

Since there is not always agreement about what is meant by stock control, it is necessary to begin by saying that, in this book, the term is used to mean *a set of policies and procedures by which an organisation determines which items it holds in stock and how many (or much) of them it carries.*

Inventory control means the same as stock control, although some people try to make a distinction. Some prefer to include work in progress in inventory while using stock to refer only to goods in the stores. Some use inventory control to mean *scientific* stock control, presumably because it is a longer word than stock. In ordinary English the words stock and inventory mean the same thing.

One fundamental objective of stock control is to satisfy the customer, whether he is outside the organisation and is a real customer who pays for what he gets, or is inside the organisation, a user of the stores who should be regarded as a customer. Customer satisfaction results from several things. The one which particularly concerns the stock controller is the service he gets from stocks: how often he can get what he wants over the counter without the delay of waiting for delivery of a special order. A level of service can be quantified and set as a target to achieve, and the service level actually achieved can also be measured and used as an index of performance. It can be measured in several ways, some of which are described later, but the standard measure of service level is *the fraction of total demand on stores which is actually met from stock.*

STOCK CONTROL SYSTEMS AND RECORDS

But this cannot be the only objective of the stock controller. By piling up bigger and bigger stocks of everything which could conceivably be required he could certainly improve the service level. But he might bankrupt the business in doing it. It is expensive to carry stocks. With very high stocks, close to 100 per cent service might be achieved; but businesses exist to earn money as well as to provide services.

Obviously it is possible to aim at very low stocks and success of this objective would be easy enough to achieve, so long as nobody worried about the service. Balancing the service with the cost of providing the service, so as to achieve the best return on the money tied up in stock and the effort employed in handling and controlling stock, is a much more complicated matter, and this is really what scientific stock control is all about.

Management theorists often distinguish between *planning*—that is, deciding what to do and how to do it—and *control*—that is, making sure that plans work out by comparing actual performance with intention, and applying correction as needed. It would be consistent with this to use some comprehensive term like stock management or inventory management to include both stock planning and stock control. In this book, however, the usual English usage, in which the term stock control is used in the more comprehensive as well as in the more narrow sense, has been retained.

NEED FOR A SYSTEM

Market uncertainties, industrial strife, increasing cost of storage space and overheads, competitive pressures make the need for logical stock control systems more urgent than ever.

The tendency for industry to become more market-oriented, with production geared to meet ever-changing customer needs and demands, will mean an increasing number of engineering changes and a wider range of products, placing great pressure on parts supply. A 10 per cent increase in sales, say, can result in oscillations in inventory levels, at considerable cost and with considerable frustration and confusion.

Increased production leads to an expansion in the volume of data, with which existing stock control systems may be too slow or too unwieldy to cope. Similarly, a system may be unable to react quickly to sudden changes, such as those caused by disruptions in production or in supplies delivery, resulting in pile-ups of unwanted items from suppliers. A source cannot be turned off instantaneously; a supplier has made the goods and he wants to send them in.

The present climate in labour relations makes flexibility essential. A strike at even one supplier out of thousands can disrupt the entire production; one has only to think of the newspaper photographs of Ford's plant surrounded by the thousands of cars pouring off production lines — without windshields. In firms supplying components to other industries, production stoppages cause a rapid increase in the number of shortages all the way down the line.

THE RIGHT APPROACH

There is, unfortunately, no standard stock control system which would suit any business. Every company has its individual problems. Indeed, different systems may be necessary for different divisions, projects or major operations.

To devise a proper stock control system, it is essential to make a systematic and logical analysis of what is being done (and what is not being done), how it is done and why it is done in the way it is. Problems must be identified and realistic objectives established. In many instances the clarification of the problem solves the problem itself. This is one of the benefits which arise from getting people to analyse their tasks. But this may not be easy.

In large organisations, the stock control manager may be able to call on O & M, work study, systems analysis or other management services, or an outside consultant, to look into his problems and suggest ways of doing things. Such advisory services have two main advantages over do-it-yourself method study: first, it is possible for one of their employees to be assigned to the investigation full time, whereas a staff member might be continually interrupted to deal with urgent, short-term tasks; second, they have made a special study of how to investigate and improve methods. But they have to work with the stock control staff and call on their knowledge of what is being done and what the purpose of it is.

STOCK CONTROL OBJECTIVES

Systems cannot be designed realistically until system objectives have been determined, nor can performance be measured without specific standards or objectives.

A good system ensures that materials are at the right place at the right time and in the right quantity. It is probable that there are financial limitations to stock held, and that storage space is at a premium. The aim, therefore, should be to meet production and market requirements economically within those limitations. William Morris, later Lord Nuffield, boasted that stores for his works were the suppliers' lorries en route to his factory. When this can be accomplished, stock control can, perhaps, be considered efficient! Until a lorry breaks down or a strike occurs.

STOCK CONTROL SYSTEMS AND RECORDS

Objectives for stock controllers can be examined under a number of different headings; a sample listing could be:

Investment objectives

- a reduction in stock holdings
- a reduction in the variety of items held
- an improvement in the stock/sales or issues ratio
- a reduction in loss due to deterioration
- a reduction of slow moving or obsolete parts

Service objectives

- an improvement in service to production or assembly benches
- an improvement in the manufacturing cycle
- an improvement in stock availability level
- elimination of production holdups
- easier introduction of engineering changes
- better machine utilisation
- a reduction in number of machines used
- shorter delivery times to production/customers

Stock management objectives

- improved records for stock movements and stock held
- more bulking of orders for improved purchase prices
- analysis of stock by usage value to develop differing strategies
- introduction of variable order quantities and variable reorder levels
- introduction of forecasting reorder procedures
- improvement in economic order quantities

Operational objectives

- use of less storage space/work in progress
- increased productivity in the stores operation
- improvements in recruitment and training
- lower material handling costs
- lower operating and administrative costs

Organisational objectives

- reduction in seasonal and other fluctuations

- improved flow of information on design changes/future demand/specifications
- an enhancement of management information
- an improvement in overall profitability
- continual reassessment of service needs and customer satisfaction

The above set of objectives, which can be added to or reduced according to local needs, could be further subdivided into those which come under the heading of 'maintenance' and those which could be termed 'innovatory'. For example, a *maintenance* objective for service level might be:

- to maintain stock availability at between 95 and 98 per cent.

An *innovatory* objective, or one that introduces a level of change, for service level might be:

- to improve stock availability level from the low 80s by 10 percentage points, within six months.

Once the latter had been achieved, it would then fall into the maintenance category. The methods by which change is achieved will depend largely on company philosophy, management style and so on, but one useful approach is to set up project teams, whereby people from different sections/departments meet, discuss and work towards a given target within a specified time limit.

Working towards company objectives causes employees to take long-range views of their functions. A short-range view might cause a production manager, for example, to produce according to the rise and fall of the sales curve, instead of looking for trends and at seasonal variations, and developing a production programme to meet requirements over the longer term. A long-range view might stabilise production levels, causing higher total inventory but substantially lower hiring and redundancy costs, and improve industrial relations. Conversely, sub-optimisation focusing only on payroll costs, but ignoring the long-term effects, can cause fluctuating inventories. It is only possible to achieve some balance between inventory costs and production fluctuations by co-ordinating the efforts of sales, distribution, production and other departments involved.

STOCK CONTROL SYSTEMS AND RECORDS

CUSTOMER SATISFACTION

Stocks are held only to meet demands on stock: to sell to the outside customer in the case of stocks held for immediate resale, or to meet without any delay the needs of colleagues inside the firm in the case of stocks held for production or works and office supplies. But while customer satisfaction is certainly a key objective, it would be uneconomic to have no regard for the cost of achieving it. The cost of holding stock can be high. A typical figure is 15 to 20 per cent a year of the average value of stock held. Higher figures are often quoted but they seem of dubious validity unless interest rates are abnormally high. The stockholding cost figure which matters is the cost which could be saved if the item was not stocked: the marginal or direct cost of holding stock.

This can add up to a very substantial figure for a large stores. But the absolute size of stocks, or the amount of money tied up in stocks, or the cost of carrying stocks, however high they may be, are not figures to be looked at in isolation. They must be related to the demand being met by the stocks: the volume of orders and the service level, or rate of customer satisfaction, if they are to mean anything.

The stock-turn rate is a useful measure, but it must be used in conjunction with some measure of shortage rate or service level (both of these terms are explained more fully in Chapter 3 under the heading 'Controlling stock levels'), and perhaps also a measure of the cost of operating the stores and the stock control, if we are not to get a one-sided story from our performance measures. Stock levels have to be compared with sales (or issue) rates, and the lead time also enters into it. The length of time it takes to get replacements, compared with the length of time one can afford to wait, is an important factor in stockholdings.

It is a triangle:

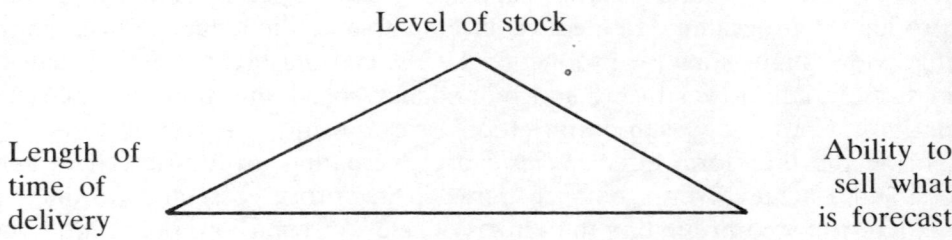

Any two on their own would make stock control quite simple. There would be no problem, for example, if a company could afford to hold unlimited stock. Or if supplies were delivered as required, or if goods were sold as forecasted.

PRINCIPLES OF STOCK CONTROL

It is the fact that these three conditions are competing against each other which gives rise to stock control problems. Delivery time may affect level of stock, for instance, and level of stock held may limit the amount which may be sold economically.

RESPONSIVENESS TO CHANGE

A good system must be flexible enough to react quickly to change, for instance, in demand or in supply. The importance of flexibility is well illustrated in the following analogy used in training courses at Kodak.

Visualise a string of army trucks ranging from personnel jeeps to heavy transports, all in a single file, one behind the other. The instructions for the front driver are to drive 25 miles an hour, plus or minus five at will, in a dead straight line. The instruction to every other driver is to follow the vehicle in front of him. One can visualise that within minutes of starting off, and as they get further and further down the queue, people are either going flat out to catch up or braking hard to avoid a multiple pile-up, simply because the reaction time from the second driver to the first, and the third to the first, and so on, gets longer and longer. Not only does the driver have his reaction time but each vehicle has its own process reaction time.

However, should the front driver be able to inform every other driver by radio every time he speeded up or slowed down, each vehicle could adjust its speed to the front vehicle. The personnel jeep would not have to take much notice because it is easy to manoeuvre. But the men in the heavy transport would benefit from not depending on the vehicle immediately in front.

In this illustration, the front vehicle is the customer ordering goods when and as he wants them. The next vehicle is the wholesaler or retailer who sells him the goods. The next one is the distribution centre which services him. The next ones are the various manufacturing or processing operation. At the end of the line is purchasing, at one moment progressing orders, the next cancelling. There must, therefore, be good radio control between the customer and the other stages. In effect, the heavy transports have a longer warning because they may have longer production times, say, or machine set up time is longer; whereas with a small vehicle, packing, for example, is more flexible. The gap between each of these vehicles, or operation, is, in fact, the buffer stock and the total gap between all vehicles is the total company inventory.

A system should not only perform routine functions, but provide quick, regular and accurate information on which decisions may be based. It could provide information, for example, on stock levels, stock movements, patterns of demand, storage capacity, financial limits, and issues for manufacturing.

Moreover, a system should be inexpensive, and the cost of it should be justified in improved efficiency and productivity. A system should be as uncomplicated as possible.

Ideally, the results should be as good as if individual attention were being paid to every stock item.

MANAGEMENT REPORTS

Reports to management should be made only if they are useful; an obvious statement perhaps, but one which is often disregarded.

Monthly reports usually give operating statistics — ratio of issues to stock, number of requisitions filed, staff employed, etc. Quarterly reports stand a little further back and may cover such matters as staff training and development, courses attended and qualifications gained, proposals for changing procedures and policies, and a general situation report: factors affecting raw materials, time lags, reducing of variety of items stocked, deliveries — particularly important now that strikes have become so much a part of the industrial scene. The annual report should be used to paint a broad picture of the department's work, its progress and future plans, together with discussion of material flow generally, how stock and inventory control policies are working out and if they ought to be altered. Informal reports, personally delivered across the desk, are more valuable than memoranda consisting largely of figures.

2

Organising the Stock Control Function

The place of stock control within the organisation will be determined by such factors as company size, policy, whether the organisation is product-oriented or manufacturing-oriented, the relative influence of the various functional managers and so on. Few firms set up stock control as a distinct department even though it may be responsible for a substantial part of the assets on the balance sheet. It is not uncommon to find stock control working under the authority of the manufacturing process, or indeed, to find that stock control is split according to the end-use of the stock. In this latter case, raw materials stock might be responsible to production, finished stock responsible to marketing, spare parts to the maintenance engineer and general, consumable items controlled indirectly by the company secretary or finance manager. This uncoordinated approach to stock management normally results in poor control, a higher than necessary investment in stock and consequential problems of stock redundancy, obsolescence and deterioration.

STOCK CONTROL AND OTHER FUNCTIONS

In some organisations the obvious link between purchasing and stock control is exploited to the full, and the concept known as the supplies manager (or supplies officer in the public sector) is applied. Under this arrangement the purchasing decisions are balanced against stock inventory needs, and hopefully the potentially conflicting objectives of each are brought together in an optimal solution. (Purchasing, for example, might want to buy in bulk in order to obtain better discounts: stock control policy, on the other hand, might require smaller and less expensively stored quantities.) In those large local authorities where central supply systems have been developed, the organisational philosophy embraces purchasing, stock service level (i.e. stock availability), responsibility, and thus stock control, under one manager. Where this integrated approach is applied, the close communication between purchasing and the stock/stores control procedures brings several other advantages:

- lead times can be monitored constantly and fed into the stock control process
- seasonality or other known fluctuations of demand can be related back to the purchasing people for appropriate action
- Sourcing problems and difficult market conditions which generate substitute materials or larger order quantities, can be absorbed more readily into the stock control system
- slow moving, redundant or deteriorating stock lines can be identified readily, but, more importantly, swift action can be taken to prevent further problems of this type
- unit loads (inwards goods) can be established so that both purchasing and stock/stores control can see benefits to either function.

MATERIALS MANAGEMENT

The most significant development in industry in this area since the late 1960s has been the growth of the 'materials management' concept. A great deal of the impetus for this development came from the USA, but also from other European countries, notably Sweden (where the concept is known as 'materials administration'). Materials management entails the total control of all purchased and manufactured goods within the organisation under a single senior manager. The reasons for this approach are many and varied but can probably be summarised as follows:

1. Manufacturing processes have advanced considerably in the recent past, and the cost reduction and efficiencies thereby resulting have now focused attention on other cost aspects of the manufacturing cycle, namely purchase cost, inventory (or stock) levels and materials handling.
2. The increasing attention paid to customer service during this same period has meant that traditional organisational structures were no longer adequate to meet the demands of the buyer's market. Departmental specialisation, with its potential for goal conflict and sub-optimisation, had to give way to a more integrated form of management.

ORGANISING THE STOCK CONTROL FUNCTION

3   The rapidly expanding use and power of computers has led to a 'total systems' facility of control. The early use of computers was characterised by a function-by-function conversion from a manual procedure to a discrete computer-based process. The current trend is to seek for a widely based and integrated approach and to use 'real time' or 'on line' computer applications, with distributed processing (i.e. separate from, but connected with, the main computer) and 'intelligent' terminals (where a degree of computing power is available locally for the non-technical user). The monitoring of materials, therefore, in what can be a complex system of movements throughout the organisation is an ideal candidate for such a form of computerised control.

Scope of materials management

The span of control that can be exercised in a materials management function will depend upon the needs of the organisation, but the following elements are normally to be found within such a system:

1   *Production planning:* the task of producing a production schedule and an analysis of material requirements. The exact method employed will vary according to the nature of the manufacturing process (job, batch or continuous production) but almost always the final outcome will be some form of materials requirements planning (MRP). The latter involves an examination of the means of manufacture, machine loading constraints, and the production of (*a*) a statement of materials, which identifies the time phasing of purchases and deliveries, taking into account stock on hand and outstanding orders, and (*b*) a production schedule which determines what will be produced given the already prepared list, or 'explosion', of requirements and machine capacities. Note that the responsibility for manufacturing does not lie within the materials management field, but is concerned with the way in which goods are produced (i.e. types of machine, labour skills etc.).

2   *Purchasing:* once the statement of materials is made available from the MRP procedure, another and logical task is the purchase of those needs. This will involve source selection, price determination, quality and delivery aspects, progressing and the contractual implications of buying and ordering. A separate, professional yet integrated purchasing section, or department, is thus required.

3   *Stock control:* the identification of stock control as a distinct (yet, once again, integrated) part of the total system. Where MRP is also part of the system, stock control is obviously closely associated with the statement of

materials, but a close watch must be maintained on the levels of available stocks and the quantities outstanding from suppliers. These latter considerations could, with benefit, be nominated for inclusion in the stock controller's job specification. Otherwise, control of non-production stocks, using past demand as a medium for forecasting, is clearly a stock control responsibility.

4   *Materials handling:* the internal movement and storage of goods entails the most effective and least-cost methods of goods handling, the safety and security of stored items, and the efficient and timely retrieval of stores for the production process (or for onward distribution of manufactured, or finished items.)

This grouping of activities under a unified system has implications for the organisation which can be far-reaching in their consequences.

Organising materials management

If the integrated approach to materials management is soundly-based for the reasons mentioned previously, and the organisation is confident that a systematic concept will improve efficiency and save money, then the management structure must be amended accordingly. The traditional departmental system of command is based on the theory of specialisms working effectively side by side; in certain types of industry, and particularly in small businesses where a powerful, leading figure draws together the various threads of specialisation and knits them into an effective unit, such a form of organisation is perfectly valid. But where these exceptions do not obtain, a way must be found to cut across departmental boundaries, and establish the idea of 'controlled flow'. In materials management terms this will normally be translated into a structure where a materials manager controls, for example:

- purchasing
- production and inventory control
- materials handling
- finished goods storage
- distribution.

The way in which this approach fits into the overall management structure is illustrated in Figure 2:1. The materials manager is either a board member or reports directly to the managing director or general manager. Thus the position is one of considerable influence, a factor that is paramount where a changeover to a total materials management system is involved. Even where

ORGANISING THE STOCK CONTROL FUNCTION

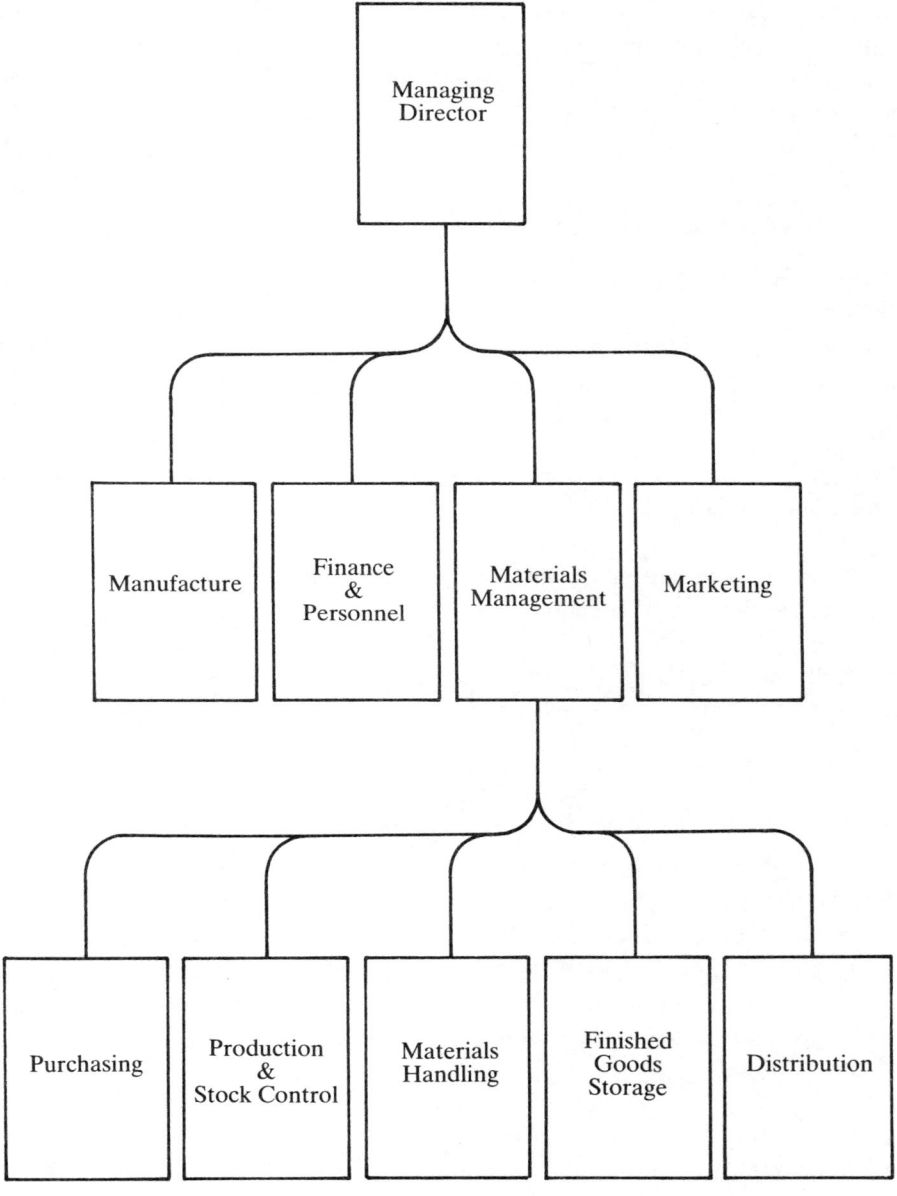

FIGURE 2:1 MATERIALS MANAGEMENT ORGANISATION CHART

STOCK CONTROL SYSTEMS AND RECORDS

the total approach is well established, the authority of a senior person in this field needs to be constantly evident, since the very nature of the flow concept of materials, from receipt to processing and through to distribution, necessarily entails a considerable geographical 'spread' in the system, crossing from one department to another, and vulnerable to interference from other pressures.

PRODUCTION AND STOCK CONTROL AT FORDS

At Ford Motor Company stock control is seen as an integral part of production planning and control. The supply of the required parts and materials for production from planned inventories is the total responsibility of manufacturing through its production planning and control organisation. Basically, production planning and control is responsible for:

- the specification of which parts and materials are required for production of the finished products

- the placing of schedules on Ford's own manufacturing departments and outside suppliers, and the calling in of that material

- establishing a relationship between the schedules for parts and materials and schedules for the machining and assembly process within its own plants.

About 6000 people are involved in materials flow control for production at Ford's seventeen plants throughout the United Kingdom. This includes all personnel involved in programming, scheduling, materials handling, stock checking and written specifications. There are about 230 parts controllers and analysts, working under a parts control manager, who are involved in detailed scheduling techniques applied to purchase parts. They develop schedules by 'exploding' parts requirements from production requirements and are responsible for purchased material coming in according to schedule, quantity and reordering.

Purchasing is not involved in stock control in any way. It is responsible solely for purchasing — selecting suppliers, negotiating prices, resolving quality problems and ensuring adequate supplier capacity.

JOB SPECIFICATION

Larger organisations, with numbers of people involved with stock control, give considerable thought to job specifications.

ORGANISING THE STOCK CONTROL FUNCTION

Job description

Dealing with queries specifically involving material movement.

Task elements. Contacting originators of movement documents, either by telephone or in person, to correct details shown on daily and supplier movement mismatched tabulations.

Knowledge requirements. Appreciation of stock file control's role in recording and correcting procedures:

> The goods receiving system and method of recording receipts, corrections to receipts, cancellations, goods received inspection system, goods received master file creation routine; factory invoicing relative to goods received.
> The factory dispatch recording system and method of recording dispatches; assembly shop inspection methods, internal order system; non-production orders, outside packers, outside machining; special considerations relative to certain orders

Skill requirements. Appreciation of the necessity for dealing with the right people at the right time:

> Ability to relate many different input documents to a complex procedure
> Ability to use an add-listing machine
> Ability to instruct users of the daily movement system in how to use the system and how to correct faults
> Ability to assess quickly the problems of processing daily movements through the computer and all possible methods of solution, and to convey accurately any pressures on the system to the data processing co-ordinator and data processing manager. For this purpose some appreciation of other pressures on data processing is essential
> Ability, through building up confidence in his appreciation of all these related systems, to exert just the right degree of pressure on the data operations manager. Speed and accuracy in handling card files and locating faulty data

Measurement criteria. Demonstrate mastery of daily movements and mis-matches by satisfactorily running daily movements for a period of not less than, say, six weeks.

STOCK CONTROL SYSTEMS AND RECORDS

Demonstrate comprehension of each factor in the daily movement system by successfully completing at least one project concerning each aspect of the problems that arise in:

The goods receiving system
The dispatch of goods system
The dispatch of goods recording system
The daily movement of raw material
The knock down recording system
Factory invoicing
Inspection acceptance and rejection procedures
Internal/non production/packers orders
The recording of spares orders and issues
Internal auditing
Scrap procedures
Salvage procedure
Shortages
The correction of error cards
Correction of invalid cards

Job description

Stocktaking.

Task elements. Appreciation of what stocktaking means:
    To the company accounts
    To the provisioning function

Competence at audit techniques, including appreciation of:
    The stocktaking system
    Alteration of stock balances

Knowledge requirements. Essential links and differences in the two aspects of company accounts and provisioning and how they are overcome.

Auditable information — its filing and retrieval and which files are affected; different methods of counting and recording; checking tallies; preparation and processing of tallies. Checking the results; use and distribution of the various tabulations, appreciation of input errors. Appreciation of processing errors.

Measurement criteria. Demonstrate a sound grasp of company's stocktaking systems and procedures during stocktaking and subsequent corrections and investigations, and where necessary explain them to the company's external auditors.

3

Application of Basic Control Techniques

Since it is impossible to devote equal attention to all items of stock it is desirable to concentrate on those which are of highest value and most important to production. One extremely useful system is known variously as value-volume analysis, the *ABC* approach, Pareto analysis, and the 80-20 law. Items are ranked and classified on the basis of descending importance or value, so that maximum attention can be paid to the relatively few items which represent the most money or annual usage.

One company applies this *ABC* approach to production items. For the high usage value group which comprises fewer than 20 per cent of the number of items but in terms of cost accounts for 70 to 80 per cent of the total, the aim is nil stock: parts produced strictly as and when required. For the next group, the intermediate '*B*' group which includes 15 to 20 per cent of part numbers and accounts for 10 per cent of total usage value, some stock is carried. But stock plus orders for any item is not allowed to exceed total commitment on the current schedule. The third group comprises a very large number of items, over half of all part numbers, but cost is relatively low. Less than 15 per cent of total usage value is due to items in the third group. A somewhat rough and ready maximum-minimum based partly on demand history is in force for these parts. Stock plus orders could exceed the commitment schedule here. A few years ago nobody here seemed to have heard of Pareto, we were told, but they certainly have now. The systems are still being developed, but the ABC approach is right. On the other hand some part numbers may be in the wrong group, and this also is under review.

At Ford Motor Company every part in inventory is listed in descending order of daily usage value, once a year. Accordingly, the most stringent inventory controls are applied to those parts with the highest daily usage value, and they received the greatest amount of attention from parts control men, stock checkers and chasers.

The *ABC* method has been well proved at Ford, where between 3 and 5 per cent of its part numbers represent half of the total value of the inventory held. Ten per cent of the part numbers represent 75 per cent of total value.

In the Class *A* category, the most expensive items, stock is checked once a month and deliveries are made daily. Class *B* items are physically checked every other month and are received weekly. Class *C* items, representing a little less than 25 per cent of the parts held, are checked every four months and received twice monthly. Class *D* items, comprising about half of the parts stocked, are checked twice a year and received monthly.

Obviously the greater the frequency of delivery, the less stock is needed to be kept on hand, thereby minimising inventory and holding costs. Stock intended for production is not locked in closed stores. Every Ford plant in the United Kingdom is an open plant and no requisition needs to be submitted to obtain materials intended for production. Controls are established on a graduated basis, according to category. Stocks checks are more frequent and tolerances much tighter on *A* than on *D* categories. Discrepancies arising on items prone to pilferage are reconciled one for one on stock records, and no tolerances are allowed on such items.

Within the principle of the *ABC* method, there is considerable leeway. In this regard, the more deviation requested, according to the company's production planning and control manager, the more satisfactory it is because it is evidence of an intelligent approach. There is a danger, he feels, that expensive items are thought of subconsciously as the larger ones, which is, of course, not necessarily true.

COLOUR CODES FOR USAGE CLASSES

The *ABC* concept can be applied on a colour-coded system, by nominating a colour for each usage value category as follows:

Green for items valued at less than £20

Blue	£20 to £50
Pink	£50 to £500
Red	over £500

Minimum stock levels and recorder quantities are set for each of the four grades, based on average use and the lead time for each component. For example, minimum level for green coded items is usage during lead time plus

APPLICATION OF BASIC CONTROL TECHNIQUES

four months' average use, and the reorder quantity is set at six months' stock.

Blue coded components have a minimum level of lead time use plus three months' average use, and three months' stock is ordered. Minimum level for pink coded items is lead time plus two months' average use, and three months' stock is ordered on a scheduled delivery basis.

For the most expensive single items, red coded components, the minimum level is set at lead time usage plus one month's average use, and reorder quantities are fixed each time by the stock controller, who takes into account use, price and risk.

ANALYSIS BY COMPUTER

Computers can readily perform this type of analysis. The basic requirement is that the stock item record holds information relating to demand history and price, two items of data without which no satisfactory system should exist. The computer is programmed to identify these pieces of information, multiply them together and thus derive the usage value. The next step in the process consists of sorting the stock items according to usage value, and here the power of a computer is truly appreciated as a fast and efficient manipulator of large banks of data. A listing can then be printed out, in descending order of usage value, displaying the item (code and description), issues made in the period, purchase price, usage value and current stock level (see Figure 3:1). An additional feature can be incorporated by showing at the foot of each page, the relationship of the number of items to the accumulated turnover *to that point*. Such *ABC*, or 80/20, lists are normally run out no more than once yearly, since any work that needs to be done as a result of the listing, e.g. elimination from the stock range of 'zero issue' items etc., is necessarily of a mid- to long-term procedure. Moreover, the use of the listing as a reference document during the subsequent period reinforces the viewpoint that the relative infrequency of its production will suffice.

CONTROLLING STOCK LEVELS

Before discussing the basic control techniques for maintaining (or improving) stock levels, it is worth examining the nature of the stock control process.

The two-bin system

Whatever degree of sophistication is applied, and however complex the techniques in use, the basis of all stock control can be found in the simple two-bin system. This is illustrated in Figure 3:2 and is the way that most domestic

STOCK CONTROL SYSTEMS AND RECORDS

```
COSMOS WLST                                    STOCK ITEM FILE 80/20 LISTING
                         TOTTENHAM DEPOT    BAY J  -  TOOLS & ENGIN
  ITEM  BUY  ITEM DESCRIPTION
  NO.   GRP
 602699  1B  PADLOCK TO PASS FB KEY WITH ONE KEY 2 INCH
   1150  2E  LOUDSPEAKER VRFA
   2788  2E  CLOCK BATTERY QUARTZ 9IN WITH HINGED WALL BRACKET
   2814  2E  CLOCK ELECTRIC 9IN WITH WALL FIXING BRACKET
 602153  1B  LOCK CYLINDER ONLY FOR RIM NIGHT LATCH WITH ROSE,BACKPLA
 603791  1B  TAP SINK PILLAR FOR ROUND T/HOLE HIGH NECKED COLD CHROME
 603804  1B  TAP SINK PILLAR FOR ROUND T/HOLE HIGH NECKED HOT CHROME
   3802  2E  COOKER CONTROL UNIT DS58 WITHOUT PLUG DS/16W
 604285  1B  CYLINDER ONLY FOR WELLINGTON NIGHT LATCH
   3230  2E  CCU CONTROL SET WYLEX 601R FUSED 2-0-2-2 WITHOUT PLASTIC
   2177  2E  BATTERY SP2     1.5V
 602179  1B  LOCK RIM NIGHT LATCH CASE ONLY
 603765  1B  TAP BATH PILLAR FOR ROUND OR SQUARE T/HOLE HOT CHROME PL
   2034  2E  CASSETTE AUDIO LH 60 MIN BASF
   1397  2E  CASSETTE AUDIO C60 60 MIN AGFA
 602647  1B  PADLOCK WITH CHAIN TO PASS  FB KEY,1 KEY 2 INCH
 603739  1B  TAP BASIN PILLAR HOT CHROME PLATED 1/2 IN
   2086  2E  CASSETTE AUDIO LH C90 90 MIN BASF
 603752  1B  TAP BASIN PILLAR COLD CHROME PLATED 1/2 IN
 602257  1B  FURNITURE LEVER FOR WATERLOO LOCK NO 20
   1761  2E  SOCKET SWITCHED 13A DS/2S
 603778  1B  TAP BATH PILLAR FOR ROUND OR SQUARE T/HOLE COLD CHROME P
 604207  1B  FURNITURE ONLY FOR WATERLOO LATCH NO 10
   3672  2E  PLUG 13A ROUND PIN DS/1 FUSED 13A
```

FIGURE 3:1 80/20 LISTING (EXTRACT)

APPLICATION OF BASIC CONTROL TECHNIQUES

ISS. UNIT	CAT	JTR	ISSUES THIS YR	ANNUAL DEMAND	PURCH.PRICE OF I.U.	VALUE OF TURNOVER	STOCK LEVEL
EA	B		25938	25938	0.780	20231.64	4285
EA	B		912	912	17.860	16288.32	348
EA	B		2295	1838	7.850	14428.30	120
EA	B		1753	1753	6.870	12043.11	320
EA	B		6667	6667	1.690	11267.23	1877
EA	B	440	2607	2607	3.390	8837.73	809
EA	B	440	2572	2572	3.390	8719.08	759
EA	B		687	757	11.200	8478.40	29
EA	B		3126	3026	2.780	8412.28	332
EA	B		1148	1148	6.920	7944.16	246
EA	B		77337	77034	0.095	7318.23	5709
EA	B		4806	4806	1.510	7257.06	899
EA	B	440	2154	2154	3.080	6634.32	961
EA	B		13482	13482	0.490	6606.18	1081
EA	B		17372	17372	0.380	6601.36	1284
EA	B		4415	4487	1.440	6461.28	9
EA	B	440	2706	2706	2.340	6332.04	939
EA	B		10084	10084	0.620	6252.08	289
EA	B	440	2653	2653	2.340	6208.02	967
EA	B		2398	2736	2.260	6183.36	4
EA	B		2597	2597	2.340	6076.98	2483
EA	B	440	1972	1972	3.080	6073.76	683
EA	B		2925	2925	1.960	5733.00	300
EA	B		4558	4558	1.230	5606.34	6373

	NO. OF ITEMS	TURNOVER
TOTAL FOR THIS BAY	1174	868,681.37
TOTAL TO THIS POINT	24	205,994.26
PERCENTAGE	2.04	23.71

FIGURE 3:1 *continued*

STOCK CONTROL SYSTEMS AND RECORDS

food cupboards are operated: if shopping is a weekly procedure, then before departing for the nearest (or best value) supermarket, a check is carried out to see whether the 'reserve' packet of tea, jar of coffee, tube of toothpaste, etc., has been opened. If so, then a new reserve is purchased, and becomes the top-up quantity for the empty bin.

This approach seems simple enough, and indeed can be used most effectively in the appropriate environment (usually small stores, or where the commodity range is limited), but problems arise when stock controllers start to examine the elements of the two-bin process:

(a) what size should the bins be (the 'how much' problem)?
(b) at what point do we seek to refill the empty bin (the 'when to order' problem)?

To illustrate these aspects more graphically (and light-heartedly), picture Robinson Crusoe on his desert island with a food or fuel requirement. If he has to replenish his stock of coconuts — food and fuel in one — from the only source in the island, he has to ask himself the question: how often shall I go to the source and how much shall I bring back? If the journey is long and arduous he will want to avoid making many trips and he will therefore attempt to bring back a larger quantity each time. In stock control terms, he trades off the investment in stock and storage by minimising the (expensive) cost of reordering. His other problem is to know when to make the journey to prevent a run-out. There may be hidden dangers on the route which could delay him considerably and he will therefore err on the side of safety and leave for the coconut plantation when his stock still indicates a state of plenty.

Once again, in stock control terms the uncertainty of lead times forces the stock controller to reorder at a high level of safety margin (or when the second bin is still relatively full).

Quite obviously, the real life stores system, with its large range of goods, multitudes of suppliers and pressures on cost and investment, intensifies greatly the dual problems faced by Robinson Crusoe. Well-developed mathematical techniques can then be applied with effects which, although the details are beyond the scope of this book, are referred to in the case study focusing on the Barnet Health Authority stores, in Chapter 6.

Measuring effectiveness

An effective stock control system will need to comply with two criteria:

APPLICATION OF BASIC CONTROL TECHNIQUES

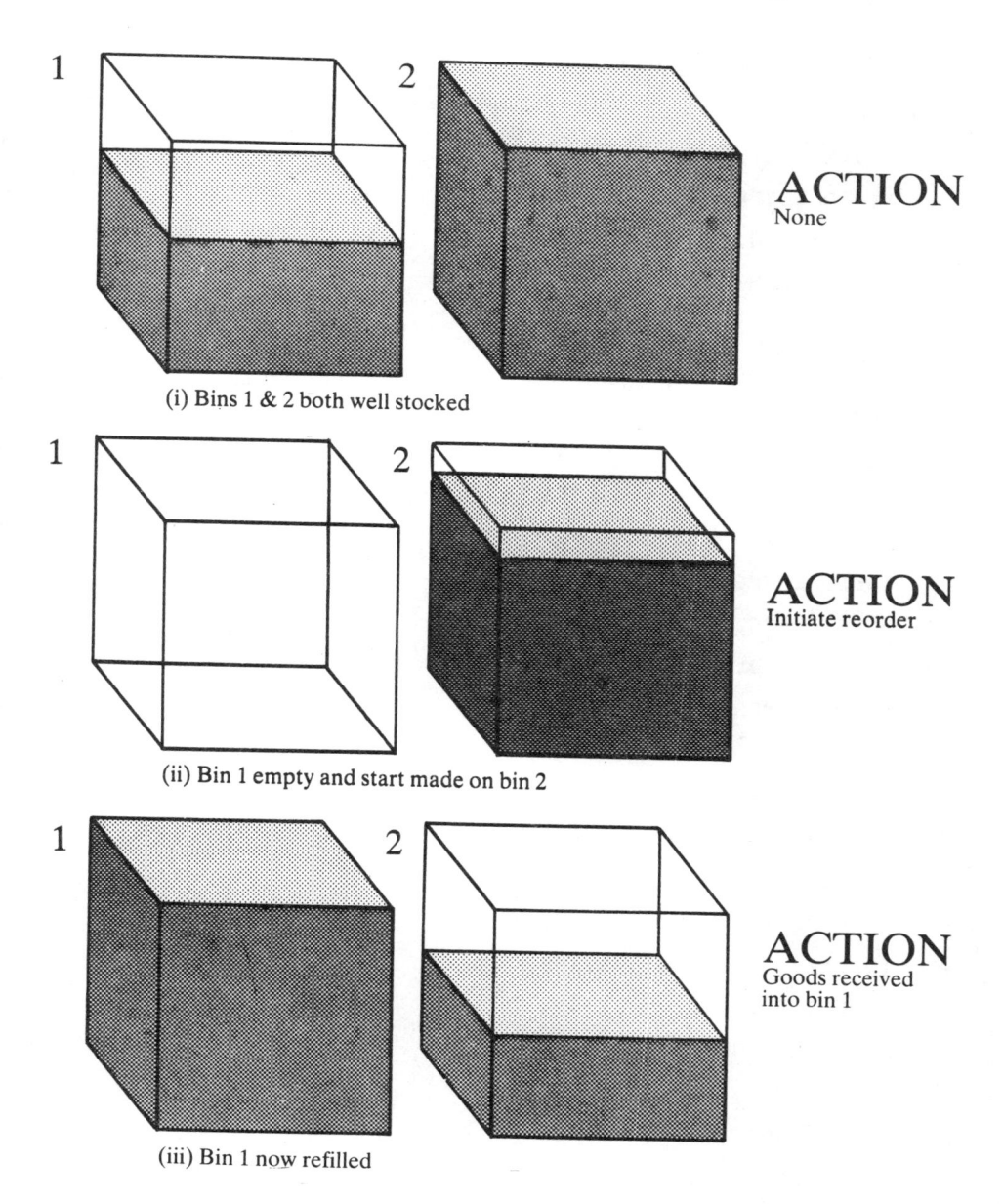

(i) Bins 1 & 2 both well stocked — **ACTION** None

(ii) Bin 1 empty and start made on bin 2 — **ACTION** Initiate reorder

(iii) Bin 1 now refilled — **ACTION** Goods received into bin 1

FIGURE 3:2 TWO-BIN SYSTEM

STOCK CONTROL SYSTEMS AND RECORDS

TOTTENHAM DEPOT

BAY	DESCRIPTION	TR/AC	NO OF PICKING NOTES	NEW REQNS SATISFIED	NEW REQNS IN ARREARS
C	CIVIL CLOTHING	453	4	12	0
E	FLOOR COVERING	452	11	12	0
G	GEN. SCIENCE	351	32	34	3
GH	CLEANING MISC.	351	0	5	0
GX	MEDICAL	351	0	88	4
H	TXT & CLEANING	451	175	127	7
HB	TURPS/SAND	356	0	3	0
HF	HOUSHLD GLOVES	451	0	14	0
HL	CLEANING AIDS	451	0	10	0
HT	TOP CLEAN	451	0	249	0
J	TOOLS & ENGIN	356	67	78	2
JA	ELECT. ACC.	356	0	20	0
JB	IRONMONGERY	356	0	18	1
JW	MISC. LAMPS	356	0	9	1
K	SHEETING/ROPES	451	2	2	0
L	HOLLOW & CROCK	354	35	237	7
M	UNIFORMS	453	30	59	2
MF	FOOTWEAR	453	0	17	2
P	INFLAM/OILS	0	1	0	0
PB	INFLAMS	356	0	1	0
Q	TIMBER	352	5	5	0
T	CLEANING TOP	0	1	0	0
TJ	TOP ENG	356	0	1	0
W	ELEC LAMPS	457	2	5	0
Z	ALCOHOLS	351	6	6	0
	NO ISSUES			3	
	TOTAL		374	1012	29

FIGURE 3:3 SERVICE LEVEL: DAILY ANALYSIS

APPLICATION OF BASIC CONTROL TECHNIQUES

TOTAL NEW REQNS	ARREARS REQNS CLEARED	DISCOUNTED VALUE OF P/NS	DISCOUNT	SERVICE LEVEL
12	1	127.90	0.00	100.00
12	3	2999.50	0.00	100.00
37	0	969.50	0.00	91.89
5	0	12.25	0.00	100.00
92	0	450.09	0.00	95.65
134	79	1439.10	0.00	94.78
3	11	70.12	0.00	100.00
14	0	69.57	0.00	100.00
10	0	106.15	0.00	100.00
249	0	1964.69	0.00	100.00
80	17	1144.23	0.00	97.50
20	0	396.42	0.00	100.00
19	14	431.85	0.00	94.74
10	0	118.02	0.00	90.00
2	0	15.30	0.00	100.00
244	0	2147.28	0.00	97.13
61	0	1020.58	0.00	96.72
19	0	758.40	0.00	89.47
0	0	0.00	0.00	
1	0	3.50	0.00	100.00
5	5	143.60	0.00	100.00
0	0	0.00	0.00	
1	0	15.60	0.00	100.00
5	0	190.30	0.00	100.00
6	0	57.20	0.00	100.00
1041	130	14651.15	0.00	97.21

FIGURE 3:3 *continued*

STOCK CONTROL SYSTEMS AND RECORDS

- the right service level
- the right investment in stock.

How right is 'right' will be for local consideration, but the means of measuring both elements will probably be based on variations of the following.

Service level

The stock controller will be judged on the success of stock availability at any one time and for that reason a measure must be found to gauge that success. On approach is to calculate the number of lines (or items) demanded against the number satisfied, and express the answer as a percentage. If this can be presented on a daily basis so much the better, and with a computerised system, the service level print-out is simply a by-product of the main processing run (see Figure 3:3).

Stock-holding

A counteracting measure is required, however, in order to ensure that the high level of service being achieved is not at the expense of an unacceptably high level of stockholding. A control-by-value procedure could be instituted, whereby the stock controller is told simply to keep stocks at or below £x. The difficulty with this method is that x needs to be constantly reviewed and revised to take into account (*a*) inflation and (*b*) changes in the rate of activity of the customer department which, in turn, affects the level of stockholding (upwards or downwards).

One popular way of relating the amount of money tied up in stocks to the demand being met by the stocks is to calculate the stockturn rate. This is defined as the average stock held over a period divided into average issues (or sales) in that period. Thus if, for instance, the period is one year, during which average stock was £20,000 and total issues from stock amounted to £80,000, the stock-turn rate would be 4. It is much more useful to know that stocks are on average turned over four times a year, or that three months' supply is held in stock (which comes to the same thing) than to know that £20,000 is the average value of stock.

An example of such a control system in practice is shown in Figure 3:4 in which the ratios are calculated and monitored three times a year.

RULED-BIN SYSTEM (FORD MOTOR CO. LTD.)

At one Ford plant that was visited, more than 7000 non-production items were being bought and plans to control such items by computer are being

APPLICATION OF BASIC CONTROL TECHNIQUES

STOCK RATIOS FOR THE PERIOD ENDING 31.12.81

0719A/28

Stock ratios are calculated by dividing the net value of issues by the average of stock valuations at close-down periods

				31.3.81	31.8.81	31.12.81	31.3.81	31.8.81	31.12.81	Minimum desired ratio	Target ratio
350	HA	Batteries	)	117	134	230	2.75	2.58	2.28	3.00	4.00
	JA	Electrical	·)	75,384	71,372	77,458					
351/8	G	Science	)	81,452	89,433	85,627	2.71	2.65	2.92	3.00	4.00
	HG	Cleaning HCL	)	554	202	308					
	Z	Alcohols		3,332	7,308	7,723	9.22	6.31	5.30	4.00	4.50
	GD	Horticulture		1,525	2,180	3,742	4.88	4.65	3.37	4.00	4.50
	GX	Medical	)	54,865	51,778	59,702	4.50	5.15	4.26	5.00	6.00
	HX	Top X	)	4,133	2,890	3,100					
352	Q	Timber		78,308	81,008	59,592	4.81	5.55	5.90	5.00	6.00
353	O	Furniture		779	700	475	-	-	-		
354	HL	Cleaning Aids	)	15,925	12,592	11,931	3.15	3.39	3.44	3.40	4.00
	L	Holloware/ Crock	))	159,367	147,104	165,434					
355/6	HB	Turps/Sand	)	4,543	3,523	6,438	3.39	3.35	4.08	3.50	4.00
	JB	Ironmongery	)	84,323	84,906	75,317					
	N	Sanitaryware	)	40,775	29,943	22,684					
	PB	Inflammables	)	2,538	1,945	1,912					
	HJ	Oils	)	87	150	145	2.92	2.93	2.72	3.00	4.00
	J	Tools & Engin	)	102,012	102,048	86,087					
	NJ	Anvils	)	492	703	642					
	P	Inflammables	)	929	852	998					
	TJ	Top Engin	)	1,738	1,598	1,424					
451	GH	Cleaning Misc	)	1,808	926	1,253	12.18	8.04	9.71	10.00	12.00
	HT	Top Cleaning	)	89,357	131,325	124,002					
	H	Textiles & Cleaning	))	94,927	110,424	93,014	5.64	3.82	5.04	5.50	5.50
	K	Sheeting/ Ropes	)	1,147	1,184	1,233					
	MH	LFB Bed Linen	)	1,190	1,726	760	13.55	13.51	16.92	14.00	16.00
452	E	Floor Coverings	))	44,236	33,647	38,459	4.44	5.33	5.10	4.00	5.00
453	C	Civilian Clothing	))	42,715	42,225	33,708	2.89	2.83	3.30	3.00	4.00
	HF	Household Gloves	))	22,630	18,475	16,679					
	M	Uniform Clothing		382,516	227,292	214,447	2.77	4.06	4.23	2.60	4.00
	MF	Footwear		106,105	75,143	63,968	1.96	2.45	2.81	2.50	3.00
457	HW	Cleaning Lamps	)	1,086	1,313	988	5.50	6.48	9.00	5.50	6.00
	W	Lamps		68,570	92,263	67,154					
	JW	Misc Lamps	)	-	10,859	11,483					
459	V	Electrical DMES		45,383	44,779	44,245	3.07	2.77	2.20	3.00	4.00
551/3		Food		452,710	546,937	590,110	16.45	20.27	17.47	18.00	20.00

FIGURE 3:4 STOCK RATIO ANALYSIS

implemented. Every non-production item is counted physically twice a year. Any item which has not moved in six months is singled out for review with whoever asked for it to be stocked, following which it is reclassified either as 'no requirement' or as stockable. Items which have not moved in twelve months are reviewed with the plant manager, whose authority is required to continue holding them in stock.

Non-production items are usually kept in a main store for each manufacturing group, with perhaps an 'expense crib' in each location where the items are mostly used. A float is worked out on the same lines as for production items for those items which could endanger production if they were not available immediately.

Stock of non-production items are controlled by establishing for each item:

A stock-turn rate
A maximum stock limit, *and*
An order level

An order level of ten working days' usage is estimated by the stores for most items. In some cases, covering cheap items, this level is shown by a bin line drawn inside the box, indicating minimum stock level; or by segregating minimum stock in a sack with a manila tag instructing stores personnel to reorder before breaking into the segregated stock.

These methods work very well and are to be preferred to keeping paper records for each transaction on each item.

STATISTICAL STOCKTAKING

Statistical sampling theory can be applied to stocktaking, in order to reduce the costly and laborious work of counting items, while still obtaining an acceptably accurate result. To be 95 per cent confident of an accuracy to 1 or 2 per cent with a parts population of 100 000 the sample size would have to be between nine and ten thousand to be valid. But this would still be costly to check on a routine basis. The Pareto principle, described at the beginning of this chapter, is used to select the sample in one firm with computerised records.

The computer first of all analyses and ranks the stock according to value and draws a line at a point to minimise the amount of effort involved commensurate with the accuracy wanted. Category *A* with 20 per cent of the parts population and constituting 80 per cent of the total value is checked thoroughly. Every item in this category is counted physically. The sampling technique is then applied to the remainder and, as these account for only 20 per cent of the total value the sample size really comes down very much.

APPLICATION OF BASIC CONTROL TECHNIQUES

As the sample is selected from the total stock record in the computer a way has to be found to take into account the stock in the store which is not on the computer. These items would fall into two types.

An item could be in the stores with absolutely no record of it on the computer. It is not shown on the TSR and therefore there is no chance of all of it being picked up in the sample. Once a month or once a quarter there has got to be a check from the stores to the TSR (total stock record) to see how often this occurs and a statistical credibility can then be put on it.

There is also the case where a part number may be recorded on the TSR; for example it could have a quantity of three recorded but in stores there could in fact be five. In choosing samples from the TSR any of the part numbers which are shown on the total stock can be chosen, but not the two which are not recorded on the TSR. One way used to get around this is to double the quantity that is on the total stock record before a sample is taken so that instead of using three for calculations, a figure of six is used so that the two in store which are not recorded in the TSR have an equal chance of being picked up with every other one. One danger is that the quantity in stock will exceed double the quantities recorded on the total stock record.

computer produces a list of part numbers and he counts them all. When these are fed back into the computer a printout will give the value of the total stock record before the check in the 100 per cent group, in the sample group and in the grand total, the value of the total stock record after the check, that is after all the anomalies have been put right, and the value therefore of the physical stock as well. It is also possible to produce details about the population, the number of part numbers in the population, the number of part numbers checked (in the 100 per cent category, all of them; in the sample, some proportion), the number of correctable errors found, and the number of errors found which are too small to be worth correcting. The computer can also produce a forecast within statistical limits of the errors that may be there but have not yet been found because only a sample has been taken.

4

Design of Stock Records

Stock records and transaction documents can be designed to:

> Record existing inventory and indicate discrepancies in stock taking
> Help to determine future demands
> Obviate reference to buried records or reliance on memory
> Reduce the need to rewrite information at different stages and each time it is processed
> Reduce queries from other departments

Manual stock records can indicate items requiring reordering, based on an established reorder level, deliveries expected, present inventory, receipts and issues, orders outstanding, etc. They can be kept in a number of places; at the actual storage location, in the stores office, purchasing office, materials control or production planning. The most comprehensive record is without value, however, unless it is kept up to date.

It is advisable to have a manual of procedures for those who are unfamiliar with the system, to ensure that data are recorded uniformly. Probably the best form for such a manual is a loose-leaf, hardcover notebook, with typewritten pages which can be detached and replaced. It should explain how the records are grouped, what systems are used for indexing each group, their location, the coding structure, the proper procedures for recording data, the procedures for transferring active files to semi-active and storage, and the period of retention. It should also contain an up-to-date list of all individuals in any way involved in the records, and should make clear their responsibilities.

DESIGNING FORMS

Before designing a form, a thorough analysis should be made of its potential function and objective, this being better than attempting a detailed alteration to the existing procedure. Colleagues should be asked for their suggestions.

Particular care should be taken to consider *complete* procedures, not just the parts of them which are carried out inside the stock control function. The aim should not be to improve stock control operations at the expense of other departments, but to improve the whole sequence of operations by making it more effective or more economical overall.

Frequency or volume is important, and both the average and the exceptional cases should be considered. HMSO publishes guide sheets which are useful in designing forms (see Figure 4:1).

The critical examination process is structured round the questions: what, where, when, who and how? The whole process and each step in the process are analysed in this way and challenged: why is that done; why in that place; why in that sequence; why by that person; why is that medium used? What else could be done instead; could the operation be relocated nearer the next operation, combined with some different activity, eliminated? What different sequence of timing could be tried? Who else could do it: someone less qualified or skilled could perhaps handle some of the detail; could it be partly mechanised? Is there an easier, safer or quicker way?

In designing a form, it is important to begin by considering how it is to be used and what specific information it is intended to provide, or what action it is intended to facilitate. The following questions should be asked:

1. What is the function or purpose of this form?
2. Why is it necessary? Is it worth what it costs to produce? Can it be eliminated? What is the worst thing that could happen if it were?
3. How else can its function be performed? Could a rubber stamp, memo or chalk entry on a blackboard be used instead?
4. Can the form be combined with another, or modified to perform a function which at present would require a second form? (Examples of this are: combination requisition/inquiry, requisition/order or order/goods receiving forms)
5. What is the purpose of each copy? Is each copy really needed?

Every word or line printed on a form, every entry made on it, must justify its inclusion. But care should be taken not to exclude features, the use of which might serve to prevent constant queries. As far as possible, forms should be self-explanatory, especially those which are used by many departments inside the organisation and perhaps by other organisations too.

Having decided what information must go on a form, the next point to

DESIGN OF STOCK RECORDS

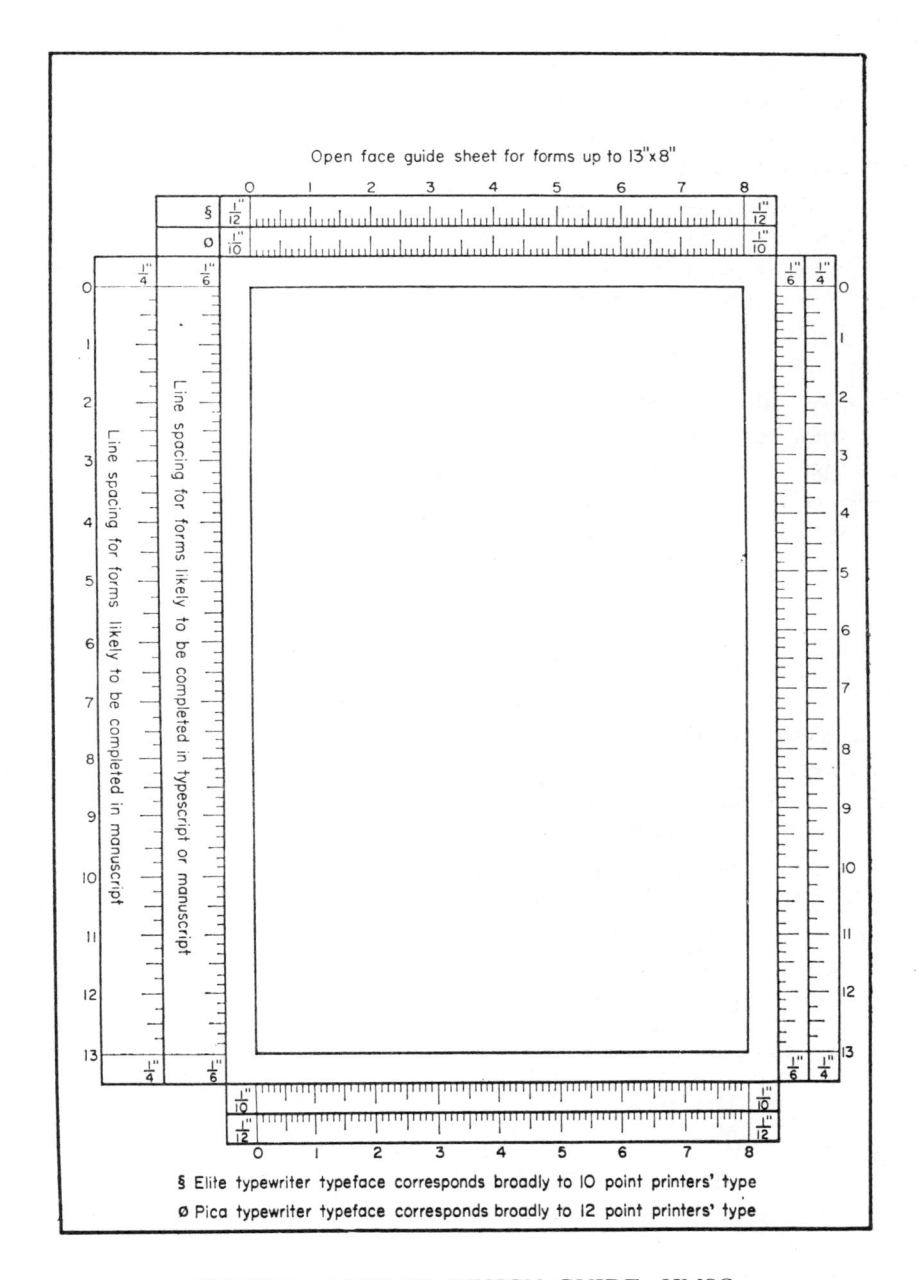

FIGURE 4:1 FORMS DESIGN GUIDE, HMSO
A handy aid to forms design is this guide sheet (Form E30) published by
HMSO
(Reproduced by permission of HMSO)

consider is layout. A clear, uncluttered, logical layout, easy to complete and easy to read, is the objective. Preferably, the form should be filled in natural sequence — that is, from left to right and from top to bottom. If the form is to be used in conjunction with another form — for instance, if data is transferred from one to the other, as is the case with requisitions and orders — the two forms should be designed together; as far as possible the relevant information should be in the same sequence and in similar locations on both documents. Fields which are always filled in are best located at the left of the form, fields which are often completed, in the middle, and fields which are seldom filled in, at the right.

This saves time in completing the form, but consideration should also be given to the question of filing. Often, when a form is filed away, the left side of it is less visible than the right, so the identification should then be at the right — or top, or bottom, or wherever; it will speed up searching for the particular document wanted. Filing margins where needed, pre-punched holes, a light rule to show where a form should be folded can all help in the disposition of forms.

Spacing of entries

It is necessary to ensure that the spacing of entries on the form is correct. Typewriting is straightforward: for vertical spacing, there are 5 lines to 20 mm, or 6 lines to 1 inch. Horizontal spacing depends on the size of type. Petit roman, the smallest type used in offices, gives 10 letters to 16 mm, or 16 letters to the inch. The two standard type sizes are elite and pica. Elite gives 12 letters to 1 inch, or 10 letters to 20 mm; pica gives 10 letters to 25 mm (1 inch). The space required for handwritten entries is obviously less straightforward. However, four lines vertically and eight letters horizontally to 25 mm (1 inch) may be taken as a rough guide.

Paper sizes

In redesigning a form, it is necessary to specify dimensions. Many forms in current use are designed to traditional British dimensions — foolscap, quarto, 8x5 in, etc. Such sizes have been all but replaced by the international standard sizes based on 1 m of trimmed paper (AO, 841x1189 mm), with the sizes which result from cutting this sheet. The standard range, with inch equivalents for the faint-hearted, is as follows:

DESIGN OF STOCK RECORDS

	MILLIMETRES	INCHES (*Approximate*)
A0	841 × 1189	33⅛ × 46¾
A1	594 × 841	23⅜ × 33⅛
A2	420 × 594	16½ × 23⅜
A3	297 × 420	11¾ × 16½
A4	210 × 297	8¼ × 11¾
A5	148 × 210	5⅞ × 8¼
A6	105 × 148	4⅛ ×
A7	74 × 105	3⅞ × 4⅛
B0	1000 × 1414	39⅜ × 55⅝
B1	707 × 1000	27⅞ × 39⅜
B2	500 × 707	19⅝ × 27⅞
B3	353 × 500	13⅞ × 19⅝
B4	250 × 353	9⅞ × 13⅞
B5	175 × 250	7 × 9⅞
C0	917 × 1297	36⅛ × 51
C1	648 × 917	25⅛ × 36⅛
C2	458 × 648	18 × 25½
C3	324 × 458	12¾ × 18
C4	229 × 324	9 × 12¾
C5	162 × 229	6⅜ × 9
C6	114 × 162	4½ × 6⅜
C7	81 × 114	3¼ × 4½

Weight, colour and surface finish of paper

The surface finish is affected by the way the form is to be completed; a matt or rough surface facilitates pencil entries; a calendered or polished surface is preferable for pen and ink; engine sized papers suit ball pens. White is the basic colour for forms, with other colours as a quck visual coding to denote recipient and facilitate sorting; but buff forms are thought by some to be less tiring to the eye for forms dealt with all day. As for weight, or thickness of paper, flimsy paper should be used only for temporary forms, not for those which have to be passed from hand to hand or filed for a considerable period.

Thicker paper should be used for permanent forms. The traditional range of weight goes from 85 grammes per square metre for legal documents and letterheads, 45 gsm for few-copy forms and 30 gsm for many copy forms. The more copies that are wanted, the thinner the paper must be if carbon or similar copying method is used. Ordinary typewriters with carbon paper can produce five to eight copies. Electric typewriters can give more copies than manual machines — as many as twelve to fifteen with thin carbon paper and thin forms.

When more than twelve copies are wanted, it is usual to prepare a master from which as many copies as are needed can be reproduced by spirit or stencil duplicator or dyeline copying. Electrostatic copiers, such as the Rank-Xerox range, are widely used when extra copies of a single order or other document are required. The reproduction method may dictate the choice of paper for the master; translucent paper is required for dyeline copying, for instance.

FILING SYSTEMS

Strip index

Perhaps the simplest filing system is the strip index, which comprises up to about 150 individual strips just wide enough for a line of typewritten information. The strips are inserted in a panel and they can be moved up or down to allow for additional strips when necessary. The strip index panels can be filed horizontally in drawers or suspended vertically on a spindle in the fashion of a carrousel (see Figure 4:2). Card strips which are wider, can be mounted in a loose-leaf binder, and are available in different colours and sizes (see Figure 4:3).

Index cards

Also simple, and one of the cheapest filing systems available, is the ordinary card index box, which can be kept on a desk top or in a desk drawer. The cards themselves are stiff enough to withstand frequent handling but flexible enough to be inserted in a typewriter. They can be sorted and divided as easily as playing cards. They are available in different colours, which can be used to identify various categories of data. The cards are also available ruled or unruled and in three sizes: 3x4 in, 4x6 in and 5x7 in, with matching boxes and dividers.

Rotary card files

Rotating wheels are useful where there is a large number of index cards which are referred to frequently (see Figure 4:4). The cards are secure and do not

DESIGN OF STOCK RECORDS

FIGURE 4:2 STRIP INDEXING

fall out when the wheel is revolved, although they can be easily removed and replaced.

Vertical wheels are available in different sizes: the smallest, for use on a desk top, contains up to about 3000 cards in a space of 1 ft^3; the largest units are floor models and contain several wheels holding as many as 30,000 cards. Figure 4:5 shows two stock control record cards designed for rotary card files.

STOCK CONTROL SYSTEMS AND RECORDS

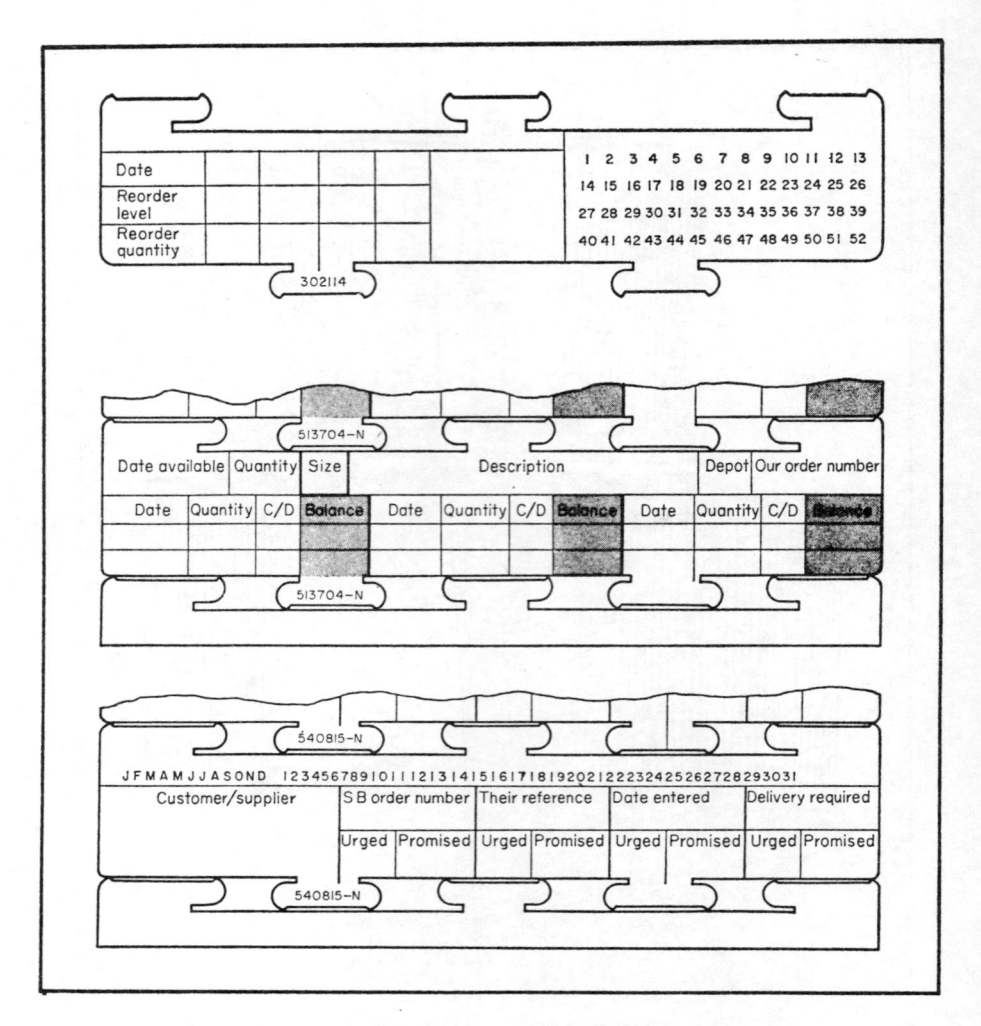

FIGURE 4:3 STRIP INDEX CARDS, KALAMAZOO

Visible edge index

With a visible-edge filing system, the forms are designed so that pertinent information is inserted on the edge for easy reference. The forms are arranged so that they overlap one another to form an index. Each form may be printed on both sides and turned. Figures 4:6 to 4:9 show forms designed by Kalamazoo for visible edge index files, including a stores record, two stores ledger forms, a form intended for analysis, and an allocation record. The

DESIGN OF STOCK RECORDS

FIGURE 4:4 ROTARY FILE

columns on each of the forms continue on the reverse side.

Figures 4:10 to 4:12 show visible edge forms designed for filing in flat trays. Such forms are usually printed on heavier stock and secured at the top edge. All makes have cellulose or acetate protective strips across the leading edge to prevent fluff adhering or tears. The trays of cards are in mobile segments and can be detached and laid on a desk (see Figure 4:13). Alternatively, the whole unit can be stored in a trolley for easy transport. Entries often have to be made by hand. Expansion and contraction of the file for inserting of withdrawing cards is usually slow and inconvenient. Frequent changes can be avoided, however, by filing cards in chronological or numerical order. If there are no changes in order sequence, it is also possible to have the reverse side of each card relate to the next card facing, so that all the information on one item can be seen without one having to keep turning the card.

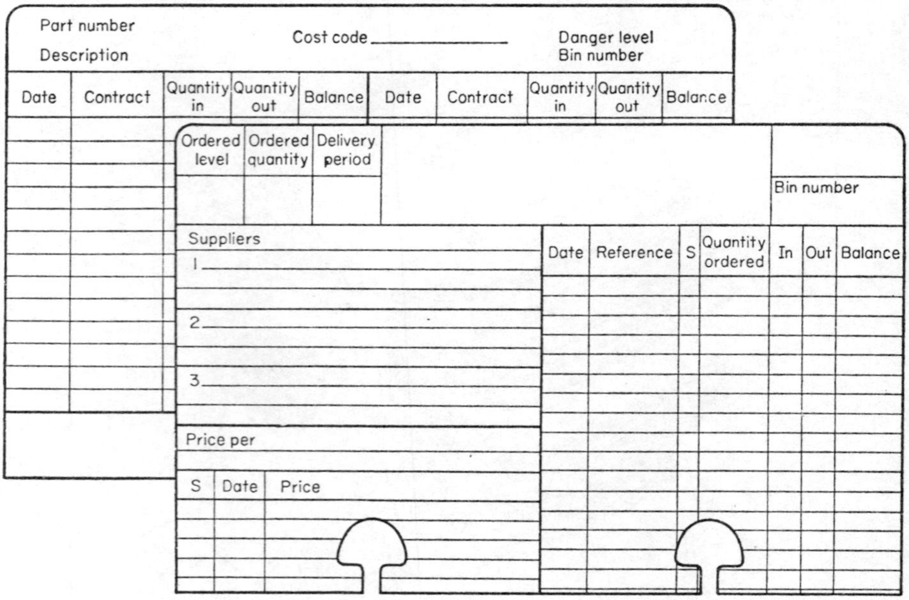

STOCK CONTROL SYSTEMS AND RECORDS

FIGURE 4:5 ROTARY INDEX FILE CARDS, C W CAVE

Hand-operated sorting systems

Forms printed on heavy stock may be coded by holes punched in the body or the edge of the card and selected by means of spindles or rods.

There are three main types, slotted, notched, and edge-punched cards. In all three types, holes are punched in predetermined spaces to designate any characteristics by which the cards may be sorted. In this way, it is possible to select cards with one or several characteristics in common, the date due for example.

In the first type, the holes are slotted in the body of the card. The features are represented by 'positions between two holes'. The holes are then connected to form slots about 10 mm long, if the items recorded on the card possess the features represented by the positions. The advantage of this type over the others is that the slot allows the cards to fall, but they cannot fall right out of the pack. They remain in the proper place. The cards are placed in a cradle, the spindles are inserted as required and the cradle is then inverted so that the cards fall upside down (see Figure 4:14). When the cradle is brought back to its normal position, the selected cards are upstanding and the pertinent information is visible from the top of the rest of the pack.

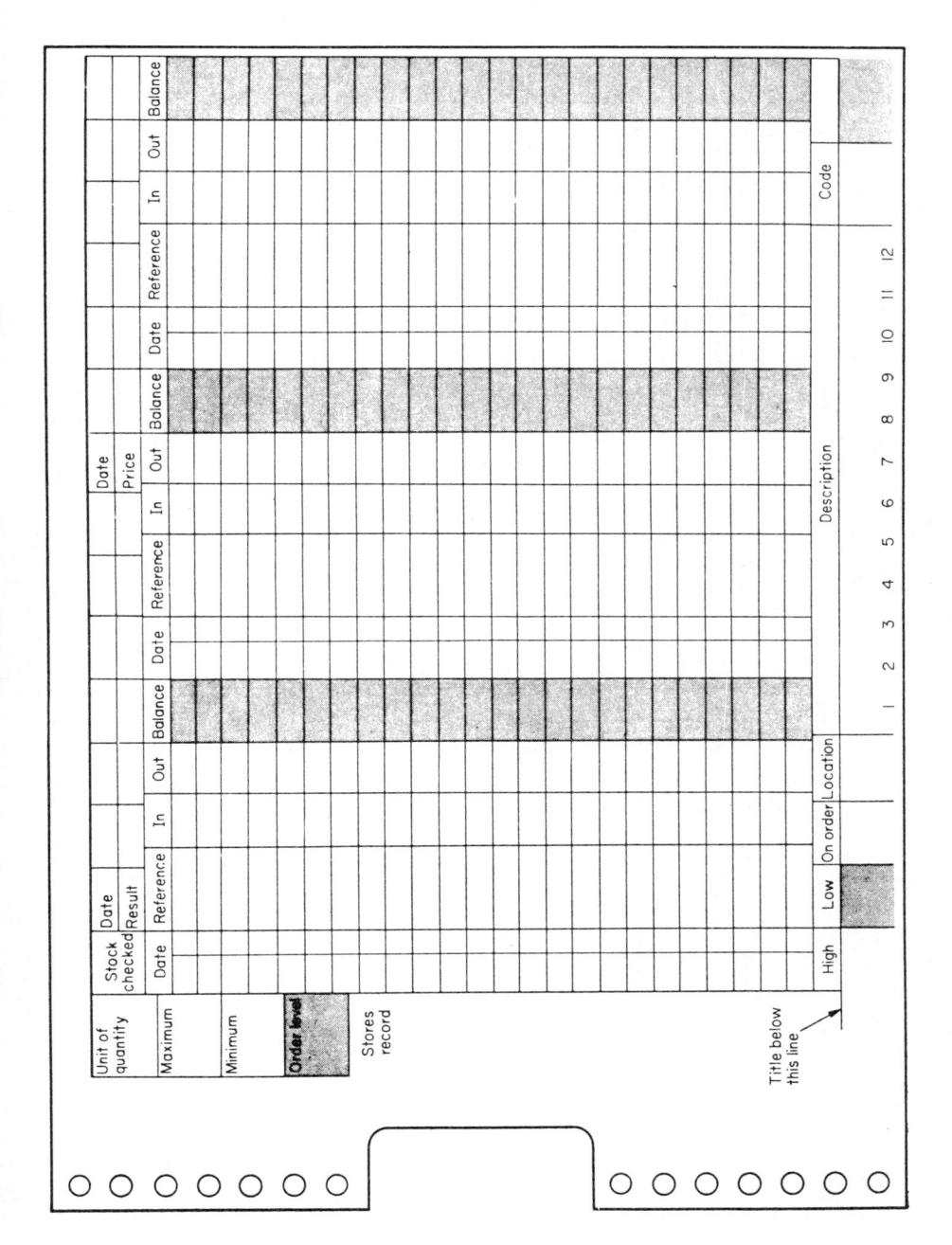

FIGURE 4:6 STORES RECORD VISIBLE-INDEX CARD, KALAMAZOO

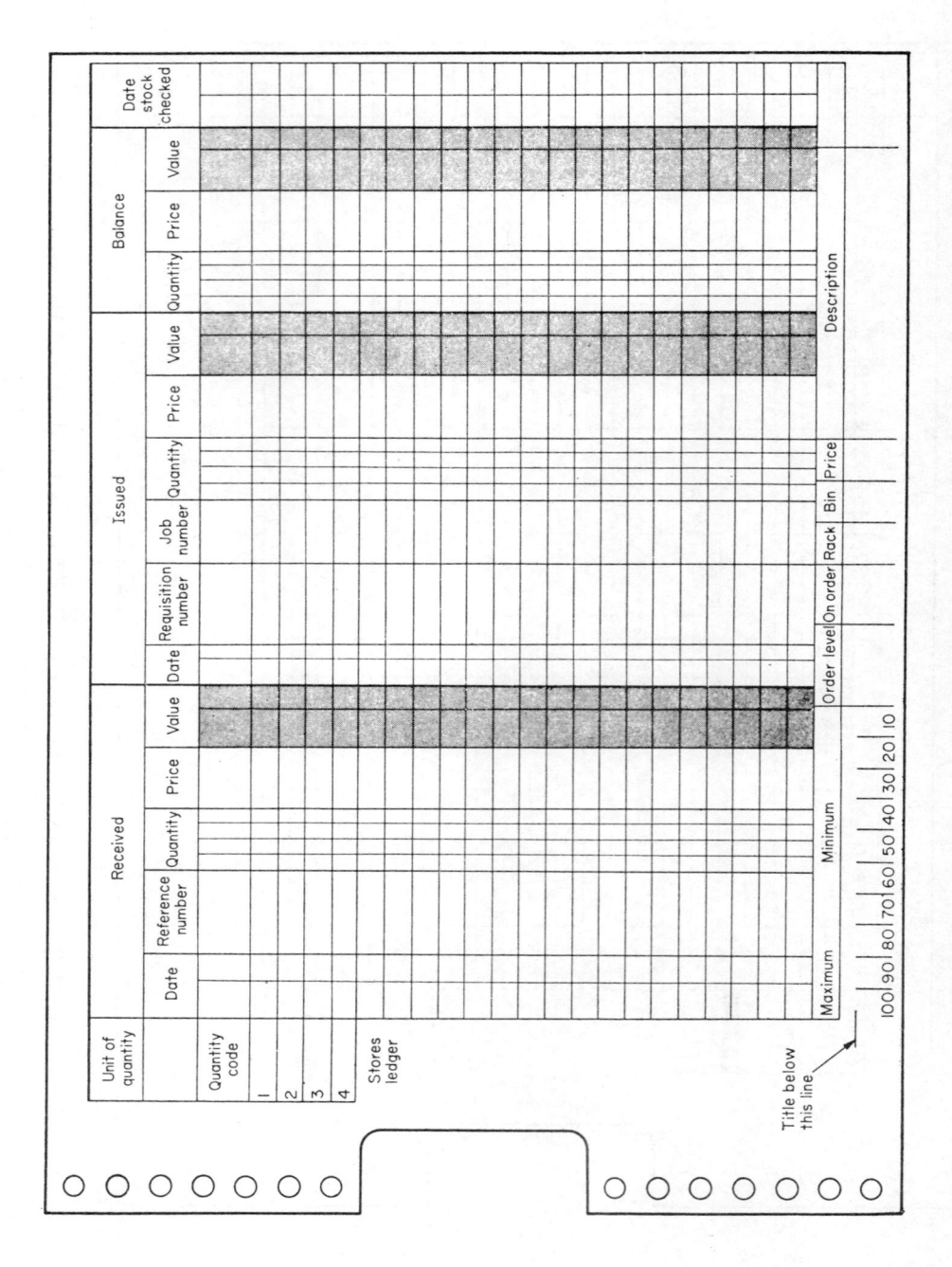

FIGURE 4:7(a) STORES LEDGER VISIBLE-INDEX CARD, KALAMAZOO

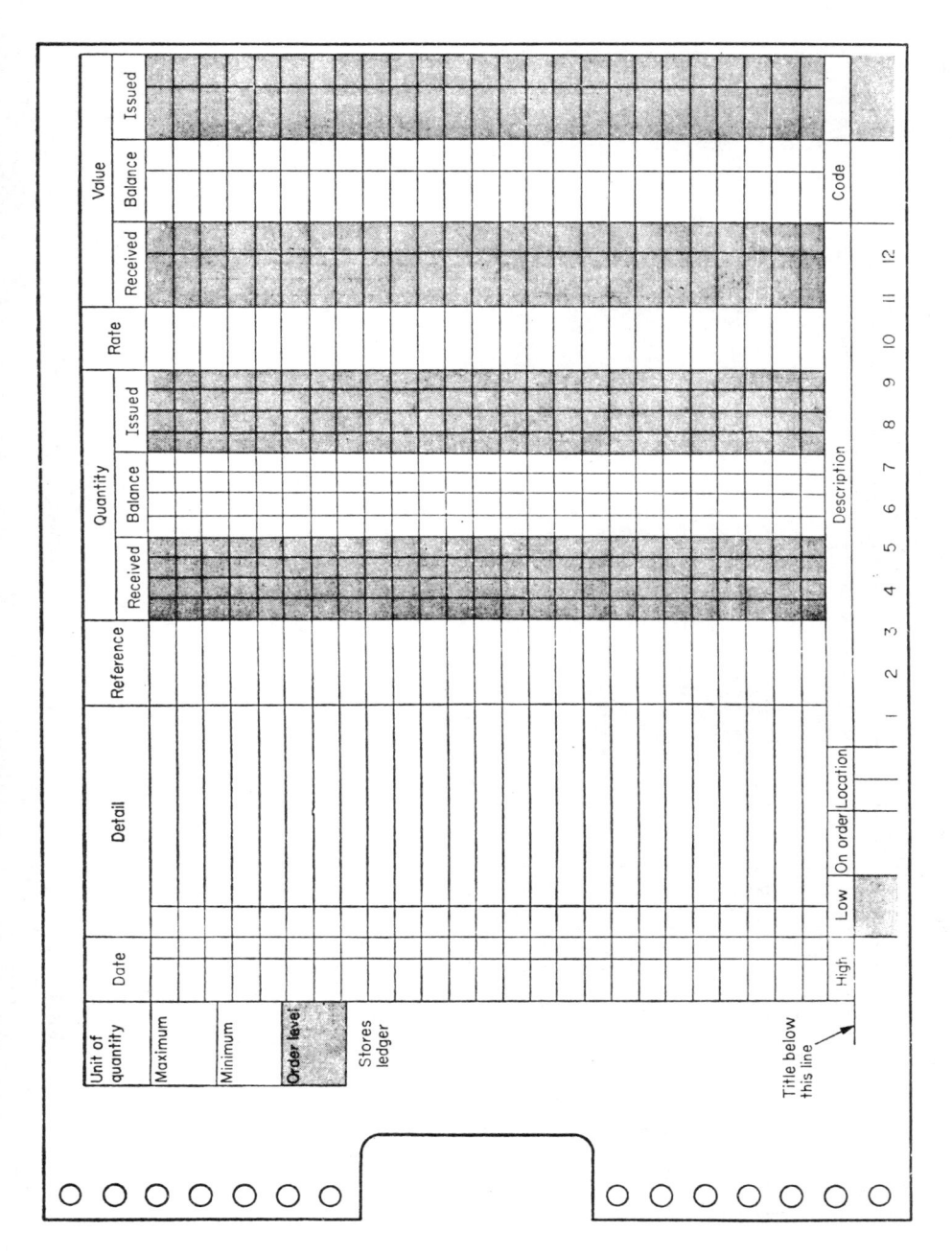

FIGURE 4:7(b) STORES LEDGER VISIBLE-INDEX CARD, KALAMAZOO

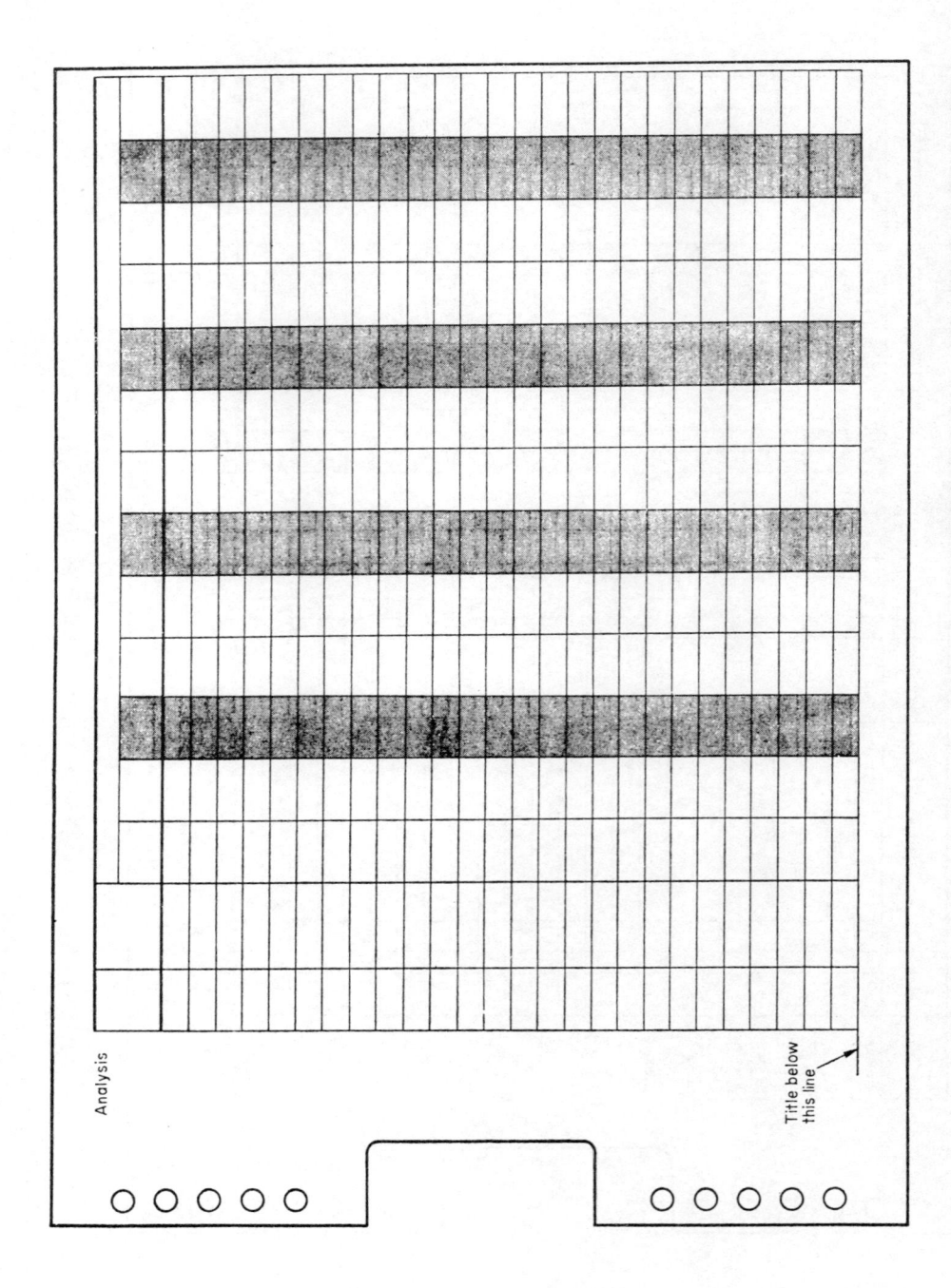

FIGURE 4:8 STOCK ANALYSIS VISIBLE-INDEX CARD, KALAMAZOO

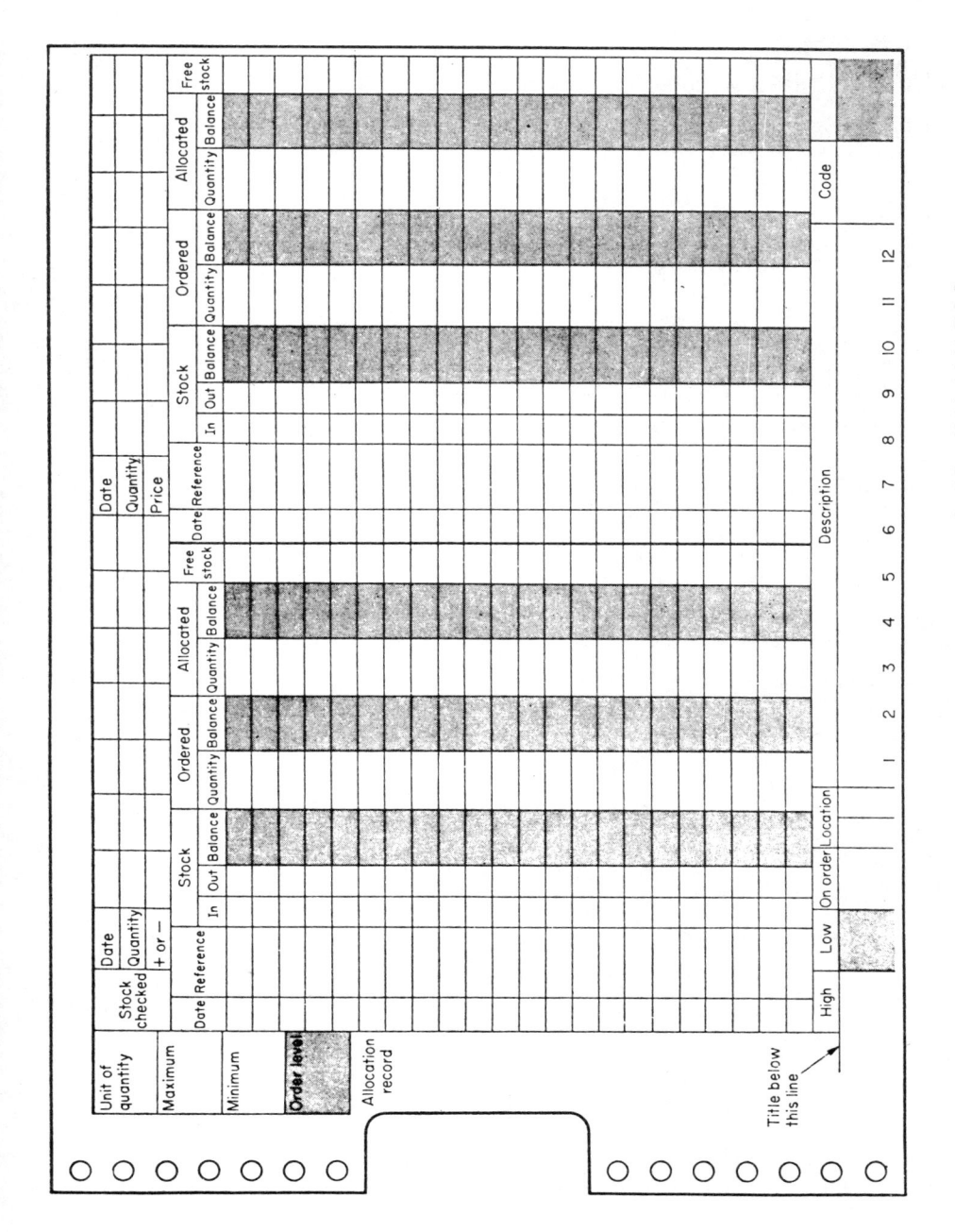

FIGURE 4:9 ALLOCATION VISIBLE-INDEX CARD, KALAMAZOO

STOCK CONTROL SYSTEMS AND RECORDS

FIGURE 4:10 STOCK BALANCE RECORD CARD, KARDEX

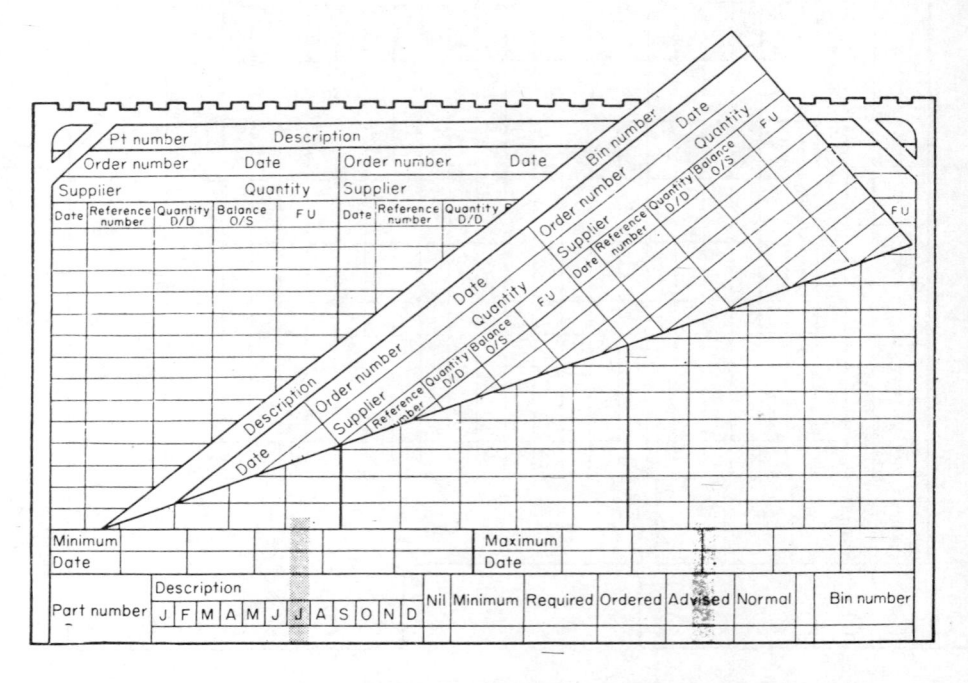

FIGURE 4:11 VISIBLE-INDEX CARD WITH OVERLEAF, KARDEX

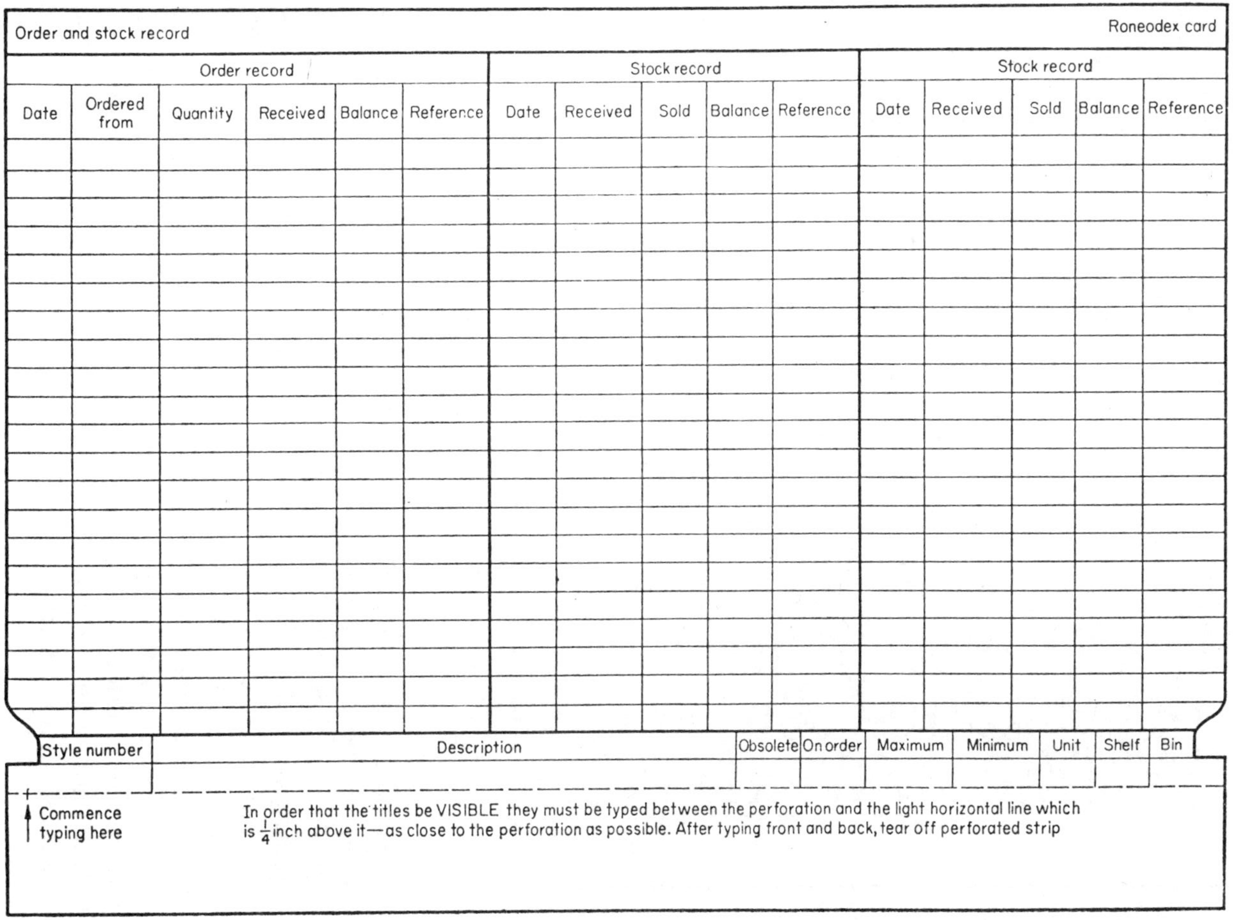

FIGURE 4:12 ORDER AND STOCK VISIBLE-INDEX RECORD CARD, RONEO

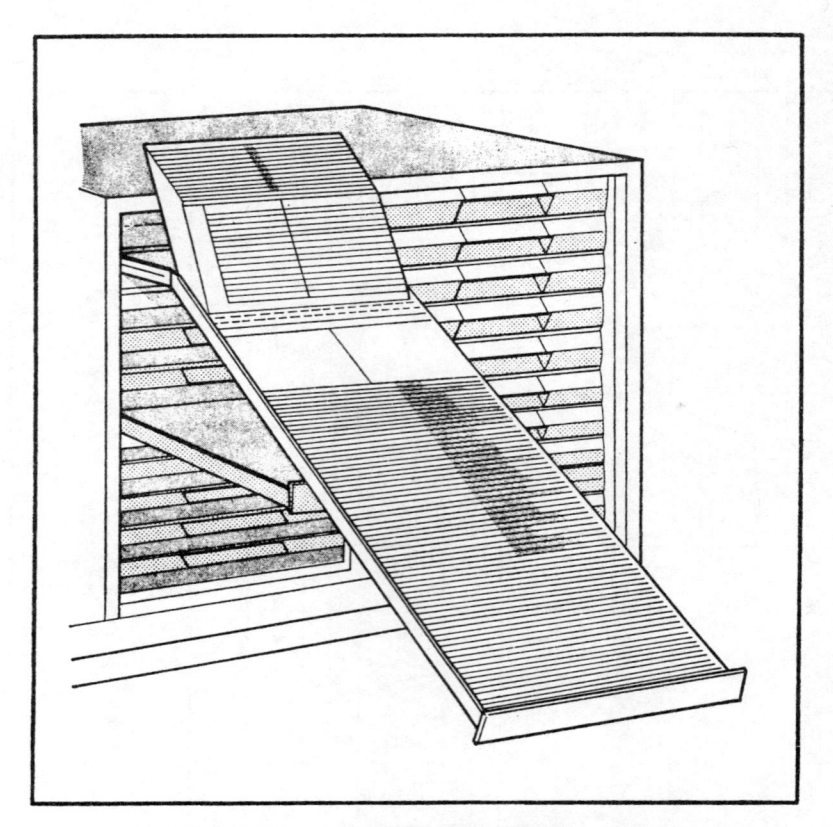

FIGURE 4:13 VISIBLE-EDGE FORMS TRAYS

In the second type, the features on the edge of the card are clipped (see Figure 4:15). A rod is then inserted in a jogger, which vibrates the cards, causing the desired ones to fall into place. Only those cards notched where the rod is situated will fall. If several rods are inserted through the pack, only those cards notched in every position corresponding to a rod will fall. In this way it is possible to isolate cards with several characteristics in common.

The third type are purchased with a series of prepunched holes on the form's edge. The holes with the desired features are slotted (see Figure 4:16). A spindle is then inserted through the pack, in the desired hole, and lifted, isolating the cards with the perforations. The process is repeated with the remaining cards, should a further division be required.

DESIGN OF STOCK RECORDS

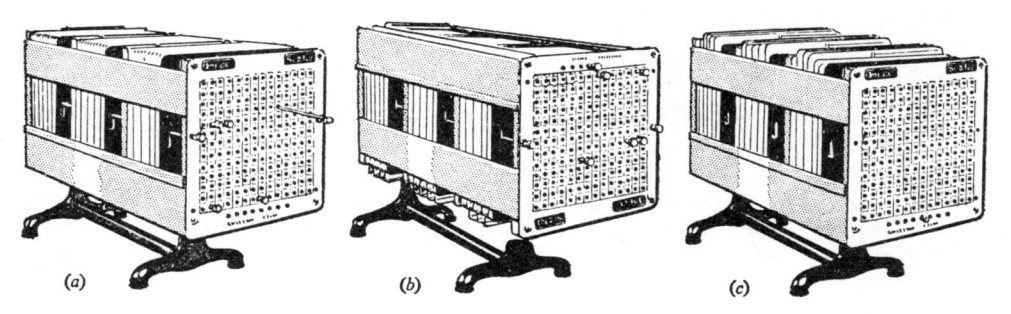

FIGURE 4:14 SELECTING SLOTTED FILE CARDS FROM THE SORTER, FINDEX SYSTEM

(a) Rods are inserted in the appropriate positions through the front plate
(b) The sorter is inverted on its cradle. The cards that are slotted in these positions will then drop down 10mm and be offset from the remainder
(c) Another rod is then inserted to lock the offset cards and the sorter returned to the upright position for easy access to the offset cards

FIGURE 4:15 EDGE-PUNCHED CARD

51

STOCK CONTROL SYSTEMS AND RECORDS

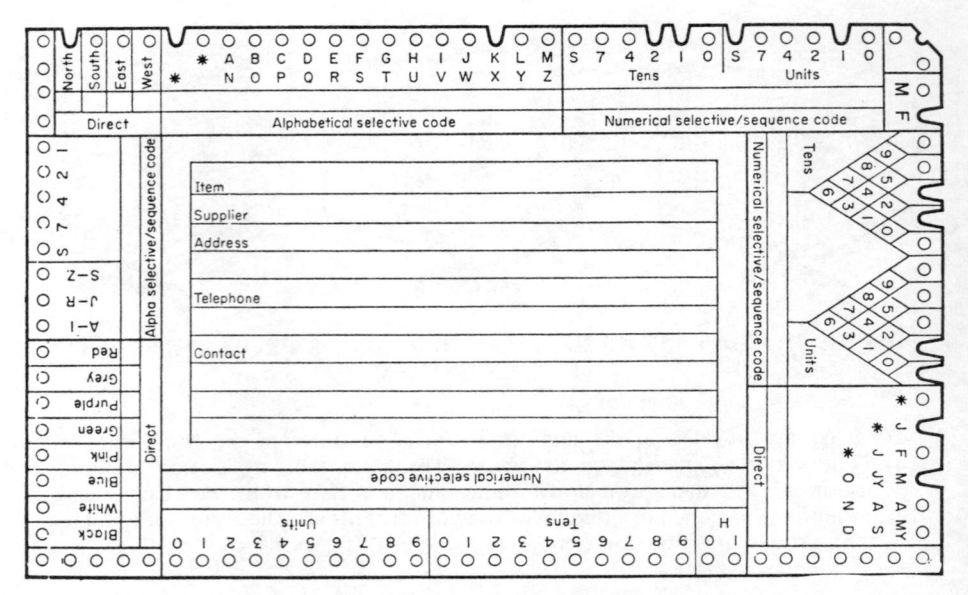

FIGURE 4:16 PREPUNCHED FORM

Microfilming

Microfilming is a method of reducing the size of documents by photography for the purpose of filing and storage. Microfilming is costly, but can be considered economical if the cost is less than the value of the space taken up for storage multiplied by the number of years for which the records are kept. Moreover, considerable time can be saved if frequent reference is made to the material.

Microfilmed documents occupy well under 5 per cent of the space required for original material, though this depends, of course, on the size of the original documents. Each reel of 16 mm microfilm measures about 80 mm in diameter and contains about 2500 exposures. Each side of a document is considered a separate exposure.

5

Computers and stock control

This chapter examines the use of computers both in general terms and as applied to stock and stores control. It begins with the history of computers, moves on to the management of an application, and ends with a suggested approach for assessing the ever-widening computer market. It concludes with two actual case studies, and a plain man's guide to computer hardware/software.

The significance of such an examination for stock controllers is the relative cheapness of computers and their local (i.e. within the stock control function) availability. This is an important development for an area of work which involves the twin pressures of service and control of investment. The ability to monitor stock closely, with rapid information retrieval and immediate action, is paramount in stock control, and remoteness of the control system is unacceptable. Thus the trend away from 'big is beautiful' and towards the placing of task responsibility in the hands of the manager is highly relevant for the stock controller in particular (see Figures 5:1 and 5:2). This implies distribution of computer processing either by using stand-alone terminals on specific mini-computers, or by establishing a corporate base of information with access to it, and control over it, by individual departments. A small-to-medium stores organisation would imply the former, and a large, multi-stores group (the RAF supply system, for example) the latter.

COMPUTER HISTORY

The computer industry has only been in existence as a force in commerce since the 1950s. The various stages of its development have each been triggered by a need for technological progress, early computers being involved in defence work whilst the American and Soviet space programmes have both provided

STOCK CONTROL SYSTEMS AND RECORDS

FIGURE 5:1 'APPLE' MINI-COMPUTER

suitable promotion in the later growth of computer techniques.

The computer industry has always been closely allied to, and has grown from, other forms of office automation, including the use of punched cards and tabulators, whilst its techniques have been adapted to such office functions as automating the typewriter and thus the production of word processing.

The unit cost of computing has progressively fallen as improvements in technology have been captured within the industry and volume of production has increased. As the size and cost of computers has been reduced together with the increase in ability of the largest computers, there has been more public awareness concerning the level of mistake and the degree of impact that this has on users. The cost of a mistake in computer usage for a small company can be disastrous today as it was for a large company in the 1950s. Most mistakes originate from mismanagement in the early stages of computer development.

COMPUTERS AND STOCK CONTROL

FIGURE 5:2 ABS MINI-COMPUTER SYSTEM

Physical characteristics

Computers look different from their early counterparts but still perform the same functions of being fed information, which is manipulated by addition, subtraction and comparison, storing some data and using it to produce reports. Initially input was by punched cards or paper tape, but it is currently predominantly by visual display units (VDUs) or as a byproduct of another activity. Storage was also on punched cards, then on magnetic tape, and subsequently on disk. Output has consistently been presented on printed forms but these can now be produced via microfilm, or microfiche, for large volumes and long-term storage. Instant response to inquiries is also available from a VDU.

Three generations of computing

The first computers were physically massive items of equipment producing high levels of heat output from their valve components. The reliability level was very low, and time taken to perform calculations (whilst very fast compared to manual techniques) was also slow compared to equipment available today. The actual power of the equipment was often no greater than that available for home computing in the current generation.

The second generation of equipment was borne on the crest of the euphoria about the transistor. Computers were still made of discrete components, thus being particularly complex items of equipment, but produced significantly less heat and required significantly less space. False flooring, massive amounts of cabling and high levels of investment were still required and the equipment could only undertake one task at a time. In these first two generations of equipment major storage was undertaken through both punched cards and magnetic tape, disk drives being in their infancy. A typical second-generation piece of equipment would be the IBM 1401, which, at its largest, comprised 16,000 (16KByte) characters of storage in its main memory, 4 magnetic tape drives, a 750 lines per minute printer and card input and card punch devices. This could also use paper tape input, but a configuration of this nature cost over £1 million (in the late 1950s) and the central processing unit weighed approximately one ton.

These items of equipment were programmed in the first generation using machine code, whilst the second generation used a one-for-one conversion process known as assemblers. This represented a major advance, since programmers could then consider computer instructions in the form of mnemonics but still had to consider the physical environment of the computer in which the programs would operate.

The third generation of equipment was able to undertake more than one task at a time, though seldom more than two, and programming could occur in 'high level' languages. These languages would typically be Cobol for business use, producing programs that could be read as an English text; Fortran would be used for scientific work, the mathematical formulae being expressed again in a readable form. This produced the concept of a true compilation of program and its careful construction. It was during this period, the early 1960s, that most of the programming techniques and standards that are used today were initially developed.

This third generation of equipment, some of which is still in use today, utilised magnetic disk in conjunction with magnetic tapes. Tapes would be used for long-term storage of information whilst the disk drives would be used in day-to-day manipulation. Card input was still the norm and batteries of key punch operators were still to be found in most installations.

Large versus small

Computing equipment grew larger and larger in terms of capabilities, while the industry began to produce smaller items of equipment, but still using the same 'batch processing' techniques. (That is, the computer would accept a group of information, such as details for invoicing, process this in isolation and produce the appropriate results.) This implied that the computer department was still a separate entity, unlike many of today's computer functions which are utilised directly by 'ordinary' company personnel in their normal daily activities.

As the size of computers became smaller the cost was also reduced. In the early 1970s the magnetic diskette was introduced, initially as an alternative medium to data preparation to produce a faster and less costly means of input to the computer system. The diskette is in appearance rather like a 7-inch gramophone record, on which information is stored, as on magnetic disk, in concentric circles of electronic blips (and is also known in some forms, as a 'floppy disk').

The advent of the mini-computer

The mini-computer was initially developed in the late 1960s and was first used for functions such as traffic systems and process control. It was introduced into commerce in an attempt to move away from a data processing department concept. One of the early UK suppliers (ABS Computers) developed special operating systems for commercial use and eventually special programming languages to place the full power of the computer directly into the hands of the user. Software, or programming, houses grew up around the mini-computer, enabling smaller companies to develop their own systems which required significant levels of man time without recruiting specialist DP personnel. The use of high-level programming languages and specialist programming languages enabled a company to undertake its own maintenance of these systems and to extend them.

The mini-computer introduced the concept of VDU input allowing direct visual communication between an operator, who has little specialist knowledge, and the computer itself. Magnetic disk became the normal means of data storage and online techniques, by having information available 'at the press of a button', became more normal. Physical size by this stage was reduced to the situation where many manufacturers had to package their equipment to look like a computer by using large boxes. The use of large-scale integrated circuitry (LSI) enabled this and also assisted in dramatic reduction of computer price tags.

Trends for the future

The developmental history of the computer has, at each stage, been associated directly with the developmental capability of electronics. The introduction of the concept of a 'chip' for storing large numbers of electronic circuits produced the next stage of computer development and the introduction of the micro desk-top computer. The industry, while still producing large mainframe computers and mini-computers, has now travelled a full circle with the introduction of the micro-computer into business and commerce with the same power as the early valve computers. Reliability is significantly increased and the computer's power is placed directly into the hands of its users, enabling stock control to be undertaken in the stores rather than in the DP department. It is also assumed that a small organisation can consider computer usage to be within its scope.

The industry is continually developing new techniques, and voice recognition together with handwriting recognition are now available to the end user. Input to a computer system can be undertaken as a direct result of writing out a customer order, and stock levels can be produced as a direct result of preparing a customer bill at a supermarket checkout.

Micro/mini — differences

Micro-computer technology is widespread throughout commerce and industry. It is revolutionising not only manufacturing processes but also the computer industry itself. Most traditional computing functions are now controlled in their own right by micro-processors. Micro-processors are found in VDU screens, printers and disk drives, while traditional central processing units are often made up of a collection of micro-processors.

A micro-processor is a complete computer in its own right reduced to a very small scale. Facilities available are obviously limited, but when combined with other items of circuitry and storage it becomes a particularly useful piece of equipment. Micro-computers are being linked together around a central filing system to provide a cost effective and powerful administration tool for the smaller business.

The distinction between a mini-computer and micro-computer, that between a mainframe and a mini-computer, is disappearing. The functions available from a piece of equipment, on the other hand, can be differentiated. Mainframes are usually used for very large-scale applications, whilst mini-computers are utilised for smaller-scale applications with online information availability. Micro-computers are used in a similar manner to minis but with smaller amounts of data and usually smaller scope for application. The situation is, however, continually changing; the facilities available on the

COMPUTERS AND STOCK CONTROL

micro are expanding, the mini-computer is growing in its capabilities and the mainframe is also increasing in size and scope.

APPLICATION OF A COMPUTER TO STOCK CONTROL

Computer-aided stock management may be an organisation's first investment in computer usage. It will, in any instance, probably represent a significant investment in computer application software, the programs to run the task. It may also represent an even more significant investment in computer hardware either added to an existing system, or a separate (possibly first) computer purchase. These tangible costs will be increased by the cost of management and staff time in determining the structure of the application and the company's own detailed requirements. This cost needs to be fully justified.

The investment decision

This overall cash investment is outweighed by the investment the company makes in its ability to manage its future. There may be limited funding available for computer purchase yet the investment will probably represent the major tool to add to administrative ability over at least a five-year period. This implies that the investment should be soundly based and thus a significant level of prior thought must be given to establishing the objectives to be achieved by the installation of a computer system.

The initial motivation to undertake computer usage could be derived from the financial planning of the company or may be the result of prior investigations into the stores status. It may result from salesmen who are aggrieved that their customers' requirements cannot be satisfied quickly, or equally from production management involved in higher overheads caused by unsuitable stores holding.

Establishing objectives

One of the objectives of computerised stores management could include an increase of profitability and whilst this may be gained from a lower stores holding and thus holding cost, it may also be gained from increased customer satisfaction and thus increased sales or reduced production cost. The techniques utilised for managing the stores, staff utilisation and the grade of personnel involved, all need to be reviewed.

STOCK CONTROL SYSTEMS AND RECORDS

The study group approach

The initial step in undertaking this task should be the establishment of a study group with direct reporting to a senior manager or to the board. One member of the study group should be assigned the major task of undertaking the research and co-ordinating the effort of the group, resulting in a formal document for consideration by the senior management of the company. The group should comprise, in addition to this senior member of staff, representatives of the variously involved company departments drawn from customer sales, production, finance and not least from the stores itself.

The person undertaking the study may be an employee of the company or he may be drawn from an outside management consultancy or the accountants/auditors. If internal resources are used there would be great benefit in consulting the company's auditors regarding their own audit requirements and for their advice regarding appropriate stores management techniques. An outside organisation can often provide objective advice which, when considered within the organisation, will extend or significantly improve the company's performance on such a project. The first part of the study will be the establishment of the objectives. Where there is more than one store involved different objectives may be established for each of them.

Factors for consideration

Factors to be considered include (amongst others specific to the organisation):

- the degree of user satisfaction from the stores
- the associated cost of non-satisfaction
- the number and type of stores
- the cost of holding stock and of purchasing lower unit quantities
- the differentiation between varying types of stockholding
- low value, high value, slow/fast moving item variations and combinations.

This should result in a renewed statement of company policy with regard to its stores holding. It is this new policy that should then be implemented within the computer system, taking into account the volumetric requirements of number of items within the stores, number of stores involved, number of different companies and branches involved, the resulting projected level of movement of stores in and out, and the principles to be established regarding stores costing techniques. A change to this last item could have a direct effect on the balance sheet in the first year.

COMPUTERS AND STOCK CONTROL

The report will also include a cost justification for the exercise which will imply that research is undertaken regarding costs of computer equipment. These can, at this stage, be broad estimates only and should be treated as having a potential 25 per cent variation. A significant level of variation on cost could be achieved by the use of a variety of costing techniques and a variety of levels of sophistication concerning the type of analysis of stockholding, the use of management and exception reporting and the type of calculation used in creating and maintaining suitable minimum stocking levels. The degree to which the standard application, if available, matches the company's require-quantities and lead times will also significantly alter the programming costs.

Competitive tendering

The final result of this evaluation should be embedded in an invitation to tender which is offered to selected computer suppliers who have suitably responded to, and assisted in the first stage of investigation. This will provide a definitive document against which the computer suppliers may tender. It will also facilitate a 'like for like' assessment at the end of the investigation phase and should ease the final task of awarding contracts. This first phase may, equally, result in the decision that a computer would not assist the company either at this time or within the foreseeable future. The company should not be afraid to acknowledge this fact and to cease its investigations at this point, combining the benefits of the study with the existing manual system to improve its efficiency.

ASSESSING THE COMPUTER MARKET

When concluding the investigation phase and commencing the task of purchasing a computer, specific criteria should be available against which to monitor response from invited suppliers. Suppliers should be asked to prepare full and detailed tenders. Any items of information requested that are refused should be considered disadvantageous to the supplier. Whilst a detailed evaluation will occur it should also be remembered that the supplier and the user will have to develop a relationship together over a number of years. The type of company, its philosophies and the personnel within the company, should not be ignored and the psychological effects of being able to 'get on together' will be important factors. It would not be unusual, in the final analysis, for the decision to be based upon these factors between two, equally competitive and suitable, possible suppliers. At this stage requests are made to meet those personnel who will develop and/or install the software, whilst meetings with the appropriate hardware engineers and other support staff from the supplier should also be arranged.

Assessment criteria

The essential criteria should then revolve around the question 'is the computer big enough?'. The second part of this question should ask 'is the computer expandable?'. Most computer systems will be expandable to some degree, although during the expansion process (as the central processing unit, or CPU, is gradually increased in its load) response times on the VDU screens and printers will deteriorate. It is the expansion level up to this point that should be established, together with any potential remedial action such as additions to the size of the CPU, its cost and method. This can result in a capital cost five-year projection in line with the company's five-year growth projection.

Another criterion is how close the supplier's offer is to the user's requirement and, in conjunction, the cost of the applications software. This can be ascertained both via written documentation from the supplier and through demonstration. During the demonstration the potential user must not be afraid to ask 'awkward' questions of his suppliers to establish the degree to which the standard application, if available, matches the company's requirements. Where a highly significant level of modification is required to a standard application, consider requesting a set of programs specially written, with the attendant costs.

The joint application software and hardware costs form the capital costs and the total of this could be from £2000 upwards. The supplier should however, be willing to accept a single contract for both items even if, as is normal practice, the application software is subcontracted by a computer manufacturer or the computer supply is subcontracted by a systems house. The protection available to the user from a single point of supply is critically important. If a supplier is unwilling to provide a single contract, this should be considered a negative point in the total evaluation.

Maintenance and 'back-up'

The hardware will require maintenance from time to time, including preventive maintenance. The response time and cost of this should be established. The response time will normally be judged from the time a call is made to the engineering services to the arrival point of the engineer. Since the computer is going to be an integral part of the management of the business this should be as short a time as possible (say 1–3 hours). A reporting procedure should be available which gradually, without the user's intervention, brings in more experienced, or more qualified engineering staff to assist in rectification of a given fault. An alternative to this approach will be the replacement of the item of equipment. The other information required from a potential supplier is the average 'up time' when the equipment is available for use as calculated across numerous sites.

Existing clients

Although the size and suitability of a supplier is an important factor, his existing clients can also be considered as part of the assessment process. A client list should be obtained and references made to ensure that he is already servicing existing clients satisfactorily. Longer standing clients, together with particularly new ones, are the most suitable companies to contact. Consider visiting an existing site to talk face to face with the users. This not only assists the assessment, but also provides valuable guidance as to the problems encountered in the installation process, and can provide further food for the thinking behind implementation procedures.

THE IMPLEMENTATION PROCESS

Inevitably the introduction of a computer into any commercial function will involve the management of change. Investment in technology must be matched, therefore, by a degree of investment in the staff working in the nominated area. Fear of job loss can be a major problem, but more importantly fear of the unknown and the feeling of inadequacy that this can generate in the individual needs to be appreciated and taken into account. Job knowledge acquired over many years becomes a familiar part of a person's working life, builds confidence and commands respect. New technology, however, can bring a rapid shift in the 'balance of power' within the workforce. Experience ostensibly gives way to technical merit and manipulation: the older worker appears to be less useful than the younger, more adaptable counterpart. The skill required to handle these perceived attitudes lies in harnessing the diverse contributions of all involved, and blending them into an effective whole.

In practical terms this will mean that, from the outset, a senior person must be nominated to guide the process of computer application from start to finish. Not only will this ensure that equal weight and judgment will be given to the competing pressures of rapid technical advance whilst retaining the established ethos, or philosophy of the organisation, but the staff in the function can be reassured about the pace of change and their status within it.

Secondly, communication should be of the essence. At every stage all reasonable measures must be taken to communicate the nature of the new process, the degree of change that it will bring, the training and planning aspects of the application procedures, and discussions (in detail with individuals where necessary) of the effects that a computer system will have on staff members. The options open in this latter aspect will depend largely on the type of organisation, but for those individuals who either would not be capable of adapting to such change or who have no desire to, voluntary redundancy, job retraining or even job creation, could number amongst them.

Thirdly, training of staff in the new system will be an obvious, although sometimes skimped, part of the implementation phase, The degree of training will depend not only on the individual concerned but also on the nature of a person's job in relation to the intended procedures. There may be a fundamental and complete change in this respect, or only a peripheral involvement: it would be wasteful, and possibly counter-productive, to overtrain where only an appreciation, or an ability to retrieve information, is required.

Throughout all these various stages there will almost invariably be the debate over job grading and pay rewards associated with technological change. It can be a many-sided debate ranging from skill replacement (VDU operators for typists) or job enlargement (more money demanded), through to an increase in an individual's marketability. An example of the latter would be the rapid development of word processing whereby a typist with the relevant ability could become a highly sought-after technician practically overnight, with attendant pay implications. It is in this area especially that the presence of the senior manager can ensure that conflict is avoided, or minimised, and if necessary, that personnel policies are suitably amended.

The actual changeover to a computer system normally entails a period of 'parallel running' in which the present procedures are maintained to perform the function whilst the computer is used to simulate the results had it been fully in use. This prodcedure has two advantages: it reveals errors in the computer system, and it develops user confidence, although clearly too much of the one will adversely affect the other!

Finally, the computer supplier should not be underestimated in the help he can give during this critical stage, but remember that although any chosen supplier should have significant levels of expertise in stores handling he will need to become familiar with each individual company. The computer supplier is an expert in computing and the user company is the expert in its own activities; it is the merging of these two factors that will result in a successful installation, although a word of caution is appropriate here in terms of this relationship. The supplier/user contact, close though it should be during the development of a computer system, must become an 'arm's length' process once installation is completed. Failure to part company at this stage can involve undue dependency and cost.

TO SEPARATE OR TO INTEGRATE?

There would probably be many functions within a company that require computer assistance, some of which may already have expertise whilst others may be in the process of research. This implies, at an early stage, that discussions should occur with the departments to ensure that the company spends the minimum time possible and does not create duplication. Internal company communciations techniques are not currently as well advanced as might be supposed and so there may be benefit in several departments sharing one computer where appropriate, whilst also ensuring that if separate computers are used they can 'talk to each other'.

Consideration to the invoicing process, financial accounting, other recording and such functions should be given during the initial investigation phase and the corporate plan should be established. This may result in the computer performing many functions on an integrated basis, so that the invoicing process finally reduces stockholding automatically. It could also result in the order taking process making stock reservations automatically.

If a computer is performing more than one function then the final management of it must also be considered. It requires the purchase of consumable items such as paper and printer ribbons, also maintenance and a certain level of security. A particular individual or group of individuals should be appointed to 'manage' the computer. They should not, however, in most small organisations be seen as computer people, but rather as a team forming the computer management function, perhaps one of many which they undertake.

CASE STUDIES

There are two case studies in this section. The first represents innovative thinking with regard to management of stocks in a retail environment, using the minimum capital investment and the maximum benefit from byproducts of this process. The second represents equally innovative thinking in terms of aiming for maximum material usage in a production environment.

Retailing study

The retailing example was initiated by the senior management of a department store in an East Anglian country town. It represented a long-standing trader in the town operating a large departmental store and two small fashion shops. A new shopping precinct was to be developed in the town and the company decided not to move into this but to compete on more traditional lines. This implied that customer service must be increased, the range of customer accounting facilities must also be increased to include budget account trading, whilst stock levels must be appropriate to customer demands. The increased level of competition in the town further implied that the utilisation of the company's financial resources must be maximised, since the shopping precinct was to bring some of the national departmental groups into the town for the first time. The company felt that it had some two years in which to consolidate its trading position and to create customer loyalty prior to the increased level of competition in an area of expanding population.

A series of detailed discussions took place within the organisation which mapped out the requirement for an integrated management and accounting application. It was decided to base this upon a small computer with the minimum of investment, but with specially prepared computer programs. Detailed research occurred within the market place in order to evaluate the most suitable potential suppliers, particular emphasis being placed upon the ability of the supplier to prepare the special programs.

The initial research enabled a budget to be established, and the equivalent of the tender previously mentioned in this chapter was communicated to suppliers verbally. Potential suppliers were selected both from the big multinational computer suppliers and more localised companies.

The system requirement included nominal ledger, sales ledger, budget accounting and purchase ledger together with implied stockholding calculations and forecasts of budgets for the procurement of new stock items. It is impossible, in a retail environment, to retain accurate figures of stockholding without individual line coding and point-of-sale accounting, although it was decided by the company to minimise their investment in accounting and other equipment. Thus point-of-sale terminals were not adopted, but products were grouped according to departmentalised structures and overall accounting undertaken. Control of the individual level of stocks was to be left to departmental buyers. The object was to retain a knowledge of the value of stocks in each section of each department. Receipts of stocks were recorded through a purchase order routine, in value terms at selling price. Sales of stocks were then captured from the cash register and credit sales recording. The periodic stocktaking details were used to establish knowledge of pilferage etc., whilst initial estimates of pilferage and other losses were included within estimated overall mark-ups. The company could thus project its purchasing requirement over a two-year period and adjust budgets during this time to reflect the sales pattern, while managing its mark-up and profitability in an efficient manner. The whole of the stock management exercise was thus undertaken as a byproduct of the other routines that require computerised assistance, i.e. financial management and purchase management. A total investment of approximately £30 000 (at 1980 values) on a single-user small business computer provided a significant improvement on the company's administrative control, its management capability of each department, and its stockholding.

Production stores study

The second example of computerised use in stores management involved a manufacturing organisation in heavy engineering. The stocks management was, again, undertaken as a byproduct of another requirement. The company required the ability to manage its progress chasing through a heavy engineering press shop for the various orders it received, maximising press and man power utilisation and minimising the lead time from commencement to completion of jobs. One integral portion of this was the management of sheet metal raw material stocks and record keeping for subsequent off-cuts.

A detailed tender was drawn up by a business systems analyst operating on behalf of this section of a large multinational organisation. The specification required the computer to be installed in the press shop and to be totally self contained, thus offering individual departmental computing facilities without reliance being placed upon computer technicians. Administrative staff enter the basic data of customer orders, stock movements and finished goods status. The foremen enter details of progress through the press shop and also have capacity to make multiple inquiries regarding the status of given jobs, machines, machine totals and other items that affect their management of the work in progress.

The press shop system keeps a record of all orders required and the materials needed for their completion. A stores system is retained which records all items in the store, and which matches the requirements of incoming orders against stores holdings. Orders are placed on suppliers for sheet metal raw material where needed. This portion of the system was organised to be relatively unsophisticated in order to gain immediate acceptance by first line management and factory floor foremen so that they could fully understand and operate the system. Much of the stores activity represents procurement against a given job, though some stockholding is maintained. In the pressing process large holes are cut into pieces of metal and the resulting off-cuts are utilised for smaller pressing hobs. The system therefore contains records of all off-cuts, details being available to factory floor operatives for matching against small pressing jobs, and thus making use of off-cuts which would otherwise have been sold as scrap. The saving from this part of the system was significant.

The third element of stores management that was undertaken within this development was that of machine tools management. The cutting tool used in the presses will successfully cut many thousands of times, but then needs regrinding. Special machine tools are often purchased for specific jobs. An initial estimate was made that the machine tool store contained 16000 items; after initial implementation of the system this was reduced to 8000, the balance having been identified as redundant tools. These were then sold for scrap, realising much capital previously tied up. Constant monitoring is now undertaken of machine tool utilisation to ensure that regrinds are undertaken when required and that redundant machine tools are not retained within the organisation. The whereabouts of any machine tool can also be established and jobs can be scheduled for utilisation of a given machine tool. This further improves the through flow of the factory floor.

Summary

These two examples are given since they involve somewhat unusual concepts of stores and stock management, representing a sort of manipulative power of computers over and above traditional stores management techniques which are discussed elsewhere.

The initial development for both of these installations was undertaken by Medoc Computers Limited of Nottingham on different items of computing equipment; the installation, in each instance, being handed over to non-technical staff for subsequent running of the computer system.

THE ELEMENTS OF COMPUTER SYSTEMS

The computer industry has an abundance of jargon, most of which is irrelevant or inconsequential for the first time user provided that certain basic concepts are present within the computer. The most important factor about the computer hardware will be the aspect of capacity to undertake the task.

'Hardware' is the term given to the physical pieces of equipment that constitute a computer, whatever its size or complexity. A normal, medium-sized computer will consist of the central processing unit (in which are stored the main 'memory' banks and logic devices that enable the computer to carry out its calculating function), a magnetic tape drive which transmits data to the central processor and a printer, which is used to turn computer information into the printed word. If a large volume of data is required to be stored for a future occasion, or if a lengthy file of, say, stock records is needed as a source of constant reference, then the computer system will also include a 'disk drive' which enables the user to store data in much condensed form.

'Software' is the name for the programming features of a computer. The hardware is inert until it is put into use by the list of instructions that are fed into it by a computer programmer. Thus a programme will tell the computer where to find the appropriate data (the number of the tape or disk, for example), what calculations to perform, and what will then need to be stored or printed. A further distinction can be made between this type of software, that is the 'application' software, and 'systems software' which is incorporated into the computer by the supplier and which governs the manner in which the pieces of hardware relate to each other, and the way that the computer's logic processes take place.

There are three fundamental requirements: information input to the computer; storage of that information; and subsequent retrieval and presentation (visually or on a printout). There must be sufficient capacity for each of these functions to occur without disruption to the business yet at an economical cost.

Input capacity

Data input will, at this stage in computing history, be through visual display screens (VDUs) or even direct-entry hand-writing recognition systems. Magnetic or optical character readers may be used, though this is unlikely; certain retail stock situations will use bar coding on product labels and light pens to read these codes.

A simple calculation can be performed with regard to visual display unit capacity requirement. The number of characters for each item of input is multiplied by the total number of items of input and divided by an expected operator keying rate or transaction event rate. However, if a particular screen is to be used for item issue, and issues are recorded as they occur, then sufficient VDU power must be available in order to process the transactions as they occur. If, alternatively, the transactions are to be input to the computer 'after the event' then assume 25 characters per transaction. Thus for 5000 transactions per day, 125 000 key depressions would be required to process the data and working at 3500 key strokes per hour (a slow operator speed for interactive VDUs) some 45 hours VDU time is required, indicating a requirement for 7 VDUs. This simple principle can be applied to each item of data input and the computer manufacturer in his proposal to the company should give full indication of his consideration on this point, but this should be checked by the user.

STOCK CONTROL SYSTEMS AND RECORDS

Information storage

Information to be stored on disk will probably be in fixed records for small computers. Each item will require a certain amount of space (calculated by the computer industry in 'bytes'). In establishing the amount of disk space required, each item of information to be stored should be assessed and the number of characters calculated (e.g. a stock line will require a code, description, minimum and maximum quantities etc.). The number of characters for each individual item should then be multiplied by the total number of items (for example, stock lines) to establish the total disk space requirement. The computer filing is usually indexed for fast access. To take account of this, and other space required on the equipment, the total amount of disk space, once calculated, should be doubled to ensure a reasonable size of equipment. Once the final figure has been established this must then be equated to the next unit of disk size available from a particular manufacturer.

Printing out

The printer will have equal sizing considerations, based upon the number of lines of print that are expected to be produced, again allowing this to occur within a specific period of time. Thus if, for example, a cyclical stock-checking principle is to be utilised the printer must be capable of producing this report in a short space of time since its preparation over an elapsed period of 2-3 hours would probably not allow for subsequent stock checking.

The central processor

The number of input devices, amount of storage and the amount of output can then be established. A computer processor is required in order to 'drive' the overall configuration. The size of the memory on this will be determined by a computer manufacturer, and different quotations could provide differing amounts of memory depending upon the technology used by the equipment. This computer memory could be located in a 'central processing unit' or it could be distributed throughout the system, each device having its own 'intelligence'.

The user should establish that each VDU can be used independently of all others and a feature called 'record level locking' is available. The record level lock implies that two individual VDUs can access a given stock record without one causing corruption (or interference with data), at the same time not preventing access by the other to the whole file. The term multiprogramming is, in this context, important, but it may also mean each operation can occur independently with each user of the equipment appearing to be his own master.

Programs or 'software'

The computer programs were mentioned earlier and are the most important part of the whole operation. The techniques determined for stock management should be established prior to purchase of equipment as previously discussed, and these requirements should be set against the offerings of the individual computer programs. The computer programs will each contain a set of instructions to perform particular tasks, but one suite of programs may or may not offer 'FIFO costing' whilst another may not offer ABC analysis. These requirements should be carefully checked, since the cost of modification of a standard set of programs (or a 'package' or pre-written, and thus, low cost, programs) is relatively high. The comparative costs of using a package set of programs and having programs specially written will need assessment against the company's own requirements.

Computer programs are of two kinds. The first set of programs (system software) are produced by the computer manufacturer and are used purely to communicate with the actual pieces of equipment and to convert the electronics into a computer. The second group, the application programs, provide the instructions to the computer to undertake a particular task, for example, stock valuation. These application programs should make as few assumptions as possible, allowing the user as much control as possible. They would, for example, not make assumptions about the rate of VAT to be added to the cost of a product.

Part Two

CASE STUDIES: SYSTEMS FOR SERVICE INDUSTRIES AND MANUFACTURING PROCESSES

6

Stock Control in Service Industries

The systems of stock control described so far relate either to a form of manufacturing process where materials are required against a predetermined schedule, or to a highly competitive finished goods market in which a lost sale is profit forgone.

Service industries, however, operate with a different set of pressures and objectives. Within this area fall hospital supplies, local government departments needs, retail and wholesale distribution, public transport undertakings, central government departments, hotel and catering establishments and many others in which the central purpose is the effective support of the primary unit, or, as in the case of retail distribution, where a stock failure represents a lost sale. In such activities, the profit motive is often non-existent as a driving force towards efficiency, and the target availability of stock is often subservient to ill-defined service concepts. The need for control is obvious, but refining proper and measurable objectives is even more important.

The aims of a stocking policy in this type of environment can include the following:

1 to act as the support function to a central purchasing activity, deriving the benefits of bulk buying
2 to achieve the appropriate degree of standardisation of items (and, as a by product, to communicate the organisation's policy in this respect by the publication of a 'standard list' or catalogue)
3 to relieve specialist staff (e.g. teachers, nurses, of the extra, and unproductive, task of locating sources of the materials needed to fulfil their primary roles: this objective can be further refined by the use of pre-printed requisitions, predetermined delivery times, simple receiving procedures etc.

4 to provide a range of consumables and essential requirements at all times
5 to enable the reduction of total stockholding within the organisation which otherwise would have a proliferation of stockholding points controlled by the consumer departments
6 to establish the economic use of investment and resources (standard and simplified documentation procedures — streamlined invoice-passing techniques, for example).

Typical of the concept of stockholding as a service support function are local authorities and hospital supply systems. The following case studies focus in more detail on the procedures and methods used to achieve stated, or perceived, aims.

GREATER LONDON COUNCIL SUPPLIES DEPARTMENT

The GLC supplies department buys and supplies goods and services for the departments of the GLC and for the schools and colleges of the Inner London Education Authority; it also has the power to supply any local authority or rate-supported body in Greater London; and it can trade with any other local authority outside London. A large part of the supply relationship is on a voluntary basis, therefore, and further dimension is added to the basic objectives of its supply function in that the department has to compete on price and service with other wholesalers operating in the local authority market.

The form of organisation is centred on two supply depots separated on a commodity basis. Each depot, or division, is treated as a cost centre and all expenses are met from trading revenue. All goods issued from stock carry a loading proportional to their share of the costs and other, purely purchasing activities; are charged on a transaction basis (as a percentage addition to the invoiced price). Both divisions distribute to all parts of London.

Performance measures

Each division sets its own performance measures in conjunction with the department's senior management based at County Hall, SE1. In stock control terms these measures take the form of:

1 a stock availability level
2 a delivery cycle
3 a series of stock ratios.

STOCK CONTROL IN SERVICE INDUSTRIES

These vary according to seasonality and commodity and are constantly under review: the significant point about such measures is that they exist and are monitored. Whether they are correct in absolute terms is not important since there is little comparative data in this area to indicate success or failure. The latter will be judged by the organisation as a whole, acting as a corporate body which should express its requirements according to wider-based criteria.

Within these dual and competing performance measures stock control operates as a flexible yet straightforward system. Each commodity manager, or supplies officer, is responsible for stock provisioning. This concept of a single person managing both purchasing and stock control is not uncommon in a service industry and particularly in the public sector. The practice is designed to concentrate attention on the overall benefit for the consumer, in terms of service and economy.

The stock control system

A computer record is held for each item and, amongst other things, will carry the following:

1 demand data (26 x 4 weekly periods)
2 an order point set by the buyer
3 an order quantity set by the buyer
4 details of current and past orders

The system is run overnight (off line) five times a week and processes customers' demands and notifications of goods received. Each subsequent issue generates a check for remaining stock against order point; each receipt will initiate a test against the 'dues' file. Thus, in stock control terms, the system is perpetually responsive without any review time lag.

If residual stock falls below order point, a stock replenishment notice is generated on that run and will be on the buyer's desk next morning (see Figure 6:1) By using the data referred to above the buyer/stock controller can decide whether to place an order or delay it; or to vary the order quantity up or down. The decision will be influenced by the current demand pattern, the time of the year (especially important where school terms or exams are concerned), the prevailing lead times in a particular industry, and so on. Once the order decision is taken, the system is notified, otherwise reminders will appear.

GREATER LONDON COUNCIL - SUPPLIES DEPARTMENT

PRINT OF STOCK ITEM RECORD

Except where otherwise stated, quantities in this record are measured in issue units.

Depot	Stock No.	Bay	Status	Trading A/c	Buying Group & Section	Category	Location in Warehouse	Standard Minute Value
TOTTENHAM	10302	GX	LIVE	351	2X	B	R 28	0.0163

Date: 14 JAN 1982

TO BE FORWARDED TO - TOTTENHAM DEPOT, BUYING GROUP 2 SECTION X

Description: SYRINGE HYPODERMIC DISPOSABLE WITH NO.12 NEEDLE 10ML.

Issue unit description: EA

Reason for print: STOCK REPLENISHMENT ORDER REQUIRED

DEMAND HISTORY

13 4-weekly periods in each financial year	1	2	3	4	5	6	7	8	9	10	11	12	13	Total	Average
Current financial year	40	60	117	168	260	246	210	317	55	4				1477	147
1930/81	95	323	238	275	193	86	121	107	103	60	184	51	188	2024	155
1979/80											110	138	294	542	180

DETAILS OF INPUT RECORD

Demand in current period	Pickings this year	Pickings last year
60	82	84

REORDER DATA

- Lead time: 4 wks 2 days — MAD of LT: 1 wks 3 days
- Reorder time: wks 4 days — MAD of RT: 1 wks days
- Total LT (incl RT): 5 wks 1 days — LT α
- Estimated usage: 126 — MAD of demand: 103
- Sum of errors — Comp K
- Shelf life — Service level
- SSVI — SS V α
- DSVI — DSV α
- Order Model — BI α
- Trend — Seasonality: N

ORDER POINT

- Cosmos Reorder Pt — Minimum stock: 400
- Previous Reorder Pt — Maximum stock: 800
- A
- B

STOCK LEVEL

- On hand: 394
- On order
- Reserved
- On order (comp): 320
- Deferred quantity not yet deducted from on hand
- Date comp. last advised order: 14 JAN 1982

ARREARS

- Quantity in arrears (since)
- No. of reqns. in arrears — Date of earliest

ISSUE DETAILS

- Issue Price
- Unloaded £
- Loaded £ 0.160
- Suggested £ 0.170
- Loading — Price change point
- Substitute stock No. — Substitution ratio
- Issues in current period: 60 — Issues this year: 1537
- DATE ISSUES LAST UPDATED: 14 JAN 1982
- Quantities for looking out on following days: 1, 2, 3, 4, 5, 6: 20, 7, 8, 9, 10

INDICATORS

ORDER QUANTITY

	Issue units	Purchase units
Buyer's OQ	320	4
Minimum OQ	25	1
Maximum OQ		
Economic OQ		

CONTRACT DETAILS

- Q on Contract
- Q remaining
- Review point
- Contractor's No. (orders): 318454 — Contractor's GLC Ref. — Mult RQ: N
- RQ No.: 800086 — RQ review date: 31 JAN 1977 — RQ expiry date: 30 JUN 1983
- VENDOR STATUS — Delivery date % — Quantity % — Quality %

PURCHASE DETAILS

- Purchase unit: CASE OF 80 — Net Price of Purchase unit £
- Date effective — New Purchase price £
- No. of IUs in PU: 80 — No. of order lines this year
- Joint Replenishment Group — VIDOS No.: 40004152
- VAT 1: 4 15.000 % — Date: 01 APR 1973
- VAT 2 % — Date
- Breakages/losses this year — Stock taking discrepancies

DETAILS OF PAST ORDERS

Order No.	Date of order	Status	Contractor	VIDOS No.	Q ordered	Q received	Date first/only delivery requested	GRS No.	Q delivered	Delivery date	Invoiced
318/100979	14/09/81	C	318454	40004152	320	320	19-10-81	207959	320	10/11/81	I
318/101030	09/10/81	C	318454	40004152	320	320	VURG	207451	320	27/10/81	I
318/101099	19/11/81	C	318454	40004152	320	320	VURG	209506	320	22/12/81	I

ORDER TO BE PLACED

Contractor's name and address:
GILLETTE SAFETY RAZOR CO
GREAT WEST ROAD ISLEWORTH MIDDX

- Trading account: 351 — Contractor's No. (Orders): 318454 — Delivery date
- Contractor's No. (Accounts) — Contractor's GLC Ref. — RQ. No.: 800086
- VIDOS No.: 40004152 — Quantity: 4 — Purchase unit: CASE OF 80 — Purchase unit price £
- Purchase description/catalogue reference
- Gross Contract Price £ — Discount 1 % — Discount 2 %
- Discount 3 % — Settlement Discount % — Carriage
- Accounting Code — Stock No.: 10302

FIGURE 6:1 GLC STOCK REPLENISHMENT NOTICE

STOCK CONTROL IN SERVICE INDUSTRIES

Monitoring reports

Service, or availability of stock, is of particular importance since an arrear is costly both for the distribution operation and in terms of the customer's receipt and accounting procedures. For these reasons a daily 'service level' point is provided, listing the availability level as a function of demand, commodity by commodity.

Once a week a detailed 'stock out' print is made available showing the number of customers awaiting a particular item, the total number of items in arrear and the date that the item first went out of stock (see Figure 6:2). A similar listing is also produced showing items that are low in stockholding, in order that any necessary progressing steps can be taken. The daily and weekly controls are distributed to managers further up the line.

The system is able to produce other types of control data as and when required, notably:

1 analyses of issues by commodity band (value-based)
2 price and demand indices
3 distribution by usage value (or '80/20' list)
4 slow-moving stock list
5 stocktaking sheets and reconciliation lists
6 stock valuation lists.

A combination of the above can be used to control the rate of stock turnover, and to calculate stock ratios, again on a commodity basis. A target ratio is set for each commodity and actual performances are calculated three times a year. Targets can be amended accordingly depending on levels of achievement.

BARNET HEALTH AUTHORITY SUPPLIES SYSTEM

The Barnet Health Authority operates a central supply system incorporating purchasing, stockholding and stores distribution. It serves a number of hospitals, health centres, clinics and district nursing organisations, providing all needs other than drugs and building/engineering requirements. The philosophy behind the operation conforms to the criteria laid down at the beginning of this chapter and can be summarised as service combined with economy.

The integration of all purchasing and stockholding under a single supplies officer provides the opportunity to derive the maximum benefit in supply terms in support of the health authority's primary function. Goods can either be made available on demand from stock or can be supplied direct from

STOCK CONTROL SYSTEMS AND RECORDS

```
COSMOS WARR..................................................WEEKLY LIST OF ITEMS IN ARR
      TOTTENHAM HALE DEPOT.............................BUYING GROUP 3  SECTION A
STOCK
 ITEM                         ITEM DESCRIPTION
  NO
 611097 TOWEL TERRY HAND BLUE
 611136 TOWEL TERRY HAND PINK
 611201 TOWEL TERRY HAND GREEN
 611539 TABLECLOTH SEERSUCKER 48X48 APPROX MULTICOLOUR-CAT PRICE INCORR
 611786 FLANNEL, FACE, 12 X 12 PINK
 612579 PILLOWS FOAM FILLED 30X18
 613359 SQUEEGEE FLOOR WOODEN INCLUDES HANDLE 18 IN
 613762 REMOVER SNOW 24 INCH
 615452 BROOM SOFT WITHOUT HANDLE NYLON 10X2
 616362 POWDER WASHING LOW SUDS FOR AUTO MACHINES 10 KG
 616492 POWDER DUSTBIN SPRINKLER 1 1/2 LB
 617311 STEEL WOOL ECONOMY GRADE  SUB FOR GRADES 1 AND 2
 619092 STEEL WOOL GRADE 1 FINE 1LB
```

FIGURE 6:2   GLC ITEMS IN ARREAR — WEEKLY LISTING

ISSUE UNIT	DATE INTO ARREAR	EARLIEST ARREAR REQN	NO OF REQNS	QTY IN ARREAR	QTY ON ORDER	STOCK ON HAND	LAST 13 PERIODS DEMAND
EA	26/01/82	26/01/82	1	100	788	16	2381
EA	05/01/82	17/01/82	6	124	688	0	976
EA	07/12/81	13/01/82	7	97	1088	21-	2025
EA	05/02/82	05/02/82	1	48	200	13	2179
EA	04/02/82	04/02/82	6	90	800	0	4455
EA	05/02/82	05/02/82	1	2	200	33-	2047
EA	04/02/82	04/02/82	2	14	0	1	505
EA	04/02/82	04/02/82	1	30	100	7	304
EA	04/02/82	04/02/82	4	17	583	4-	1173
EA	04/02/82	04/02/82	9	38	680	1-	5422
EA	12/11/81	12/11/81	73	1708	0	6785	24966
EA	04/02/82	04/02/82	10	54	1120	0	6195
EA	05/02/82	05/02/82	1	3	0	0	245

FIGURE 6:2 *continued*

a manufacturer or factory, depending on the nature of the item, degree of urgency, price etc.

The stores system

Some 5000 items are held in stock at any one time, ranging from medical requisites to tinned food and provisions. Deliveries are made by the authority's own transport using a matrix scheduling system (type of commodity and location) which enables consumers to know, and plan for, the exact half day on which certain goods will arrive. Depending on the type of item, the service is two or three times a week, weekly or monthly, although an emergency override is always available.

A significant proportion of requisitions are in pre-printed format, whereby the user is required to enter only the quantity needed. On receipt in the supplies division, requisitions are scrutinised for obvious errors, amended where necessary and batched for pre-posting. A mini-computer is housed within the supply centre and is used for all the stores documentation, stock control and purchase data required to run the operation.

Once posted, the computer prints out daily picking lists, analysed by use and also summarised in bulk. These are passed to storekeeping staff for the selection, packing and despatch of goods according to the schedule mentioned above.

The stock control system

The computer stock control system is capable of the automatic calculation of stock levels and recommended order quantities, based on past usage and supplier's delivery information, but only 65 to 70 per cent of items in a typical health service range are amenable to such treatment. The system therefore recognises five different categories for reordering purposes:

Y   Automatic recalculation
N   Manual recalculation (various reasons)
T   Term order (for scheduled deliveries in accordance with the requirements set out at the beginning of a contract)
S   Standing order — signifying regular deliveries
R   Redundant or obsolescent item.

Under the automatic recalculation system, a history of usage and delivery data is required before confidence can be generated in the effectiveness of the formulae: the amount of data required will depend largely on the consistency of both factors. Levels are recalculated for one commodity group each

STOCK CONTROL IN SERVICE INDUSTRIES

working day and, in addition, whenever an item falls to or below the minimum stock/reorder level. The system traps unusually high demand requests, by placing an upper issue limit of half of the reorder quantity. The user's attention is drawn to this eventuality by an indicator on the picking list; subsequent action in the form of checking back on the original requisition, or arranging a suitable delivery for the balance, can then be organised without detriment to the supply of that stock to other users.

Automatic recalculation formulae

The formulae in use to recalculate reorder levels and reorder quantities are explained below:

1 *Reorder (or minimum) level*
   The unit of calculation is usage in weeks, and the two basic elements comprising reorder level are manufacturer's lead time (MLT) and administrative lead time (ALT). The latter can be entered as a constant and represents such internal procedure as order placing, receiving, counting, putting away etc., whereas the supplier's lead time will fluctuate according to circumstances and is thus averaged on a progressive basis.

Another element is added to the MLT and ALT and is known as the safety margin (SM). This is composed of two parts representing firstly, the fluctuation of weekly demand and secondly the fluctuation of lead times (both expressed as a deviation from the average). The two deviations are added together and are calculated as a percentage of the total lead time. A further refinement is made to the calculation of these deviations however, in that only deviations in *excess* of average are used when calculating, in turn, the average deviation. For example, if average lead time is 4 weeks and actual lead times are:

4, 5, 6, 3, 2, 7 then actual deviations are:
(0) + (1) + (2) + (1) + (2) + (3) = average deviation is 1.5 weeks

But using only arithmetically positive deviations:
(0) + (1) + (2) + (0) + (0) + (3) = average deviation is 1.0 weeks

The formula for the calculation of reorder or minimum level is thus:

Manufacturer's lead time (MLT) + administrative lead time (ALT) plus a safety margin of average demand fluctuation (ADF) and average lead time fluctuation (ALT) both expressed as a percentage of total lead time.

STOCK CONTROL SYSTEMS AND RECORDS

2 *Reorder quantity*
   The reorder quantity calculation under this system does not seek to optimise the conflicting costs of storage versus reordering as in the classic economic order theory, but is rather a pragmatic solution in favour of a high service level (some 98 to 99 per cent availability). It derives originally from a concept known as the Department of Health and Social Security (DHSS) maximum average stock levels (MASLs). These suggest the appropriate number of weeks' cover for a particular commodity expressed as a percentage — thus fast-moving items are set at 5 per cent of the year's usage whilst other items could be set at a figure as high as 75 per cent. The reorder quantity is calculated as a function of maximum average stock. In the Barnet system, the use of DHSS factors has been replaced in favour of a consistent approach which simply uses lead times (multiplied by two), and the addition of the administrative lead time plus the safety margin, both of which have already been referred to above. Reorder quantity is then expressed as the maximum stock, less the safety margin and an adjustment to reflect orders on hand and goods owing to consumers.

Performance assessment

The emphasis on providing a high level of service and stock availablity obviously influences the stock replenishment process and, as demonstrated above, the inclusion of safety factors based on the careful assessment of fluctuations in lead time usage testifies to this philosophy. Nonetheless, the centralisation of stock management and the application of formula-based techniques of provisioning, aided by a dedicated computer, has enabled the authority to reduce stockholdings by half over a four-year period. Moreover, service has been considerably enhanced as a result of effective control.

Other features of the system

Once the central requirements of a stores system have been satisfied by the system design, i.e. stores documentation and stock control, other supplementary features can be written in for no more than the marginal cost of software and input and output procedures. In the Barnet system, the following are available:

- allocation of expenditure to users or budget holders
- production of daily stock movements for audit purposes
- maximum stock level excess reports
- processing of orders and control of late under/over orders

STOCK CONTROL IN SERVICE INDUSTRIES

- batching of orders to take advantage of quantity discounts
- buying history or buying information
- control of items out of stock (subsequently reprocessed on receipt of stock)
- listing of top value items for closer control
- immediate on-line access of stock records via a visual display unit for query, resolution and consumer inquiry.

MARKS AND SPENCER

Total turnover of Marks and Spencer in 1980 was £1850 million, roughly 33 per cent in foods and 67 per cent in clothing and homeware. It is important to realise that with over 250 stores, some very big, some very small, the range of merchandise varies enormously. All Marks and Spencer stores sell exclusively St Michael merchandise, but the very big units have a much greater range of it and carry the newest lines.

Marks and Spencer have been conspicuously successful in simplifying the systems which produce, in retail stores throughout the country, ready supplies of stock items varying from fresh ducks to men's pyjamas.

What is understood as stock control by Marks and Spencer would probably be called budgetary control in any other organisation. The budgetary control department is responsible for:

1. the collation of sales and stock estimates from the buying groups
2. the preparation of a company stock control plan, adjusted weekly if necessary
3. the allocation of stock targets to stores
4. the weekly allocation of merchandise from manufacturers to stores, in accordance with the stock control plan
5. regular reviews of buying group's store stock targets, which are adjusted depending on sales and production performance
6. sales and stock estimates for new stores and major extensions
7. the production of monthly records of performance compared with budgets.

The collation of the buying estimates for the board enables them to review sales, stock and production budgets every two or three months.

Efforts are made to organise production programmes so that the company's manufacturers have sufficient work throughout the year to keep their labour force busy. The loss of trained labour is therefore avoided.

STOCK CONTROL SYSTEMS AND RECORDS

The company believes that it has a pragmatic approach to budgeting and that it is important to remain as flexible as possible. Budgets are, within reason, adjusted continuously, according to the evolving sales pattern and the development of new lines.

The company's 'pipeline' of standard merchandise is as follows:

- approximately six weeks made-up goods in stores
- seven weeks on manufacturers' shelves, *and*
- six weeks in production

This stock commitment applies broadly speaking from February to October. Obviously, reaction to sales which do not come up to estimate has to be quick in order to avoid overstocks. Reaction is also quick to any new succesful line, within the constraints of the availability of materials and production capacity.

Every week the buying departments notify budgetary control of the amount of merchandise they wish to send to stores. Within a reasonable margin, these quantities are controlled to fall into line with sales estimates and predetermined stock levels. However, the company is again flexible and is content to be within 2 to 3 per cent of the total target.

Store stock targets are based on agreed total stockholdings for the end of each month throughout the year. Obviously, stock levels fluctuate from week to week, according to sales, which of course can vary considerable, depending on internal and external factors. However, if in any retail store the stock discrepancy is more than about 10 per cent, budgetary control looks into the reason for it and endeavours to bring stock back to the required level. The central distribution system receives detailed sales and stock information from all their stores, half the departments one week, the other half the next.

7

Manufacturing Processes

H W WARD AND COMPANY

Computer stock control systems are not confined to large companies with their own computers and teams of systems analysts and programmers. H W Ward and Company, a medium-sized machine tool company in the Midlands, has shown how a smaller company can use them.

H W Ward is situated at Worcester and employs about 400 direct workers. Approximately 30000 different items of steel, casting and forgings, bought and manufactured items are stocked. About 10000 of these items are stocked to satisfy service and spares requirements on non-current machine types and consequently are relatively slow moving.

Formerly, and prior to 1973, H W Ward had two main works. Apart from the one at Worcester which then employed about 1000 direct workers, they had a works at Selly Oak near Birmingham which employed 600 direct workers.

Like other machine tool manufacturers in the United Kingdom, Ward for many years manufactured a limited range of models against firm orders. When fifty number 2 capstans, say, were ordered, fifty sets of component parts were procured and fifty sets of drawings were issued, with the order of process written on the back. Being a small organisation with a high proportion of long-service employees, the company did not need more detailed planning or control; each man knew who did which job, and the administrative side was kept to a minimum. Because of the permutations in production, however, not every part in the fifty sets of material was used, and excess stock kept building up over the years. Moreover, each plant was buying small job lots and, in many cases, paying extra.

As long ago as September 1965, Ward introduced a major new product and management realised that existing stock control procedures were no long adequate, and a better system had to be devised.

An engineer was engaged and given a free hand to devise systems for stock control, machine loading and costing. An IBM service bureau was used for the detailed programming. The programs were written specifically to the instructions of the company, who told the service bureau precisely what information was required at every phase. Staff were trained in card punching and verification, to provide the weekly stock and ordering transactions to the bureau in the form of punched cards.

There were an estimated 8000 steps in setting up a programme and a master file. IBM completed the task in six months. It would have taken H W Ward perhaps two or three years. The entire system was implemented without additional staff, apart from a student engaged for a holiday period. The cost then for setting up the program and master file was £3500. Computer processing cost about £4500 a year and, if to this amount are added the costs of hiring card punching equipment and verifiers, the necessary staff, and the stationery, the whole system can be said to have been fully operational for under £10 000 each year, inclusive of the bureau charges.

Approximately two years after the system was introduced Ward had not only reduced holdings substantially but had improved the feed of parts to assembly benches and allowed materials to be bought more cheaply by placing bulk orders with suppliers for both plants. Where both plants used the same item, the plant using more of it was responsible for purchasing it and feeding it to stores in the other plant, on a monthly basis. This relieved Selly Oak of much stockholding and provided it with some badly needed space. No clerical stores records were then maintained, although more clerical staff had to be taken on for card punching and verification.

Since those early days the Selly Oaks works has closed and production has been concentrated at Worcester. In 1975 Ward transferred the programs from the IBM data bureau to an in-house IBM computer. With the previous years of experience gained by using the bureau the transfer was effected without any disruption. Today the system of control is essentially the same as described here. To return in time to the initial reorganisation which was necessary to create the method that is still applicable today, the facts are as below.

Organisation

Having analysed the detail involved, the company defined exactly what information was required and how often. A master 'stock file' was set up, containing the lead times and material cost information, together with stock balances, which would be kept up to date by posting issues, receipts, and so

MANUFACTURING PROCESSES

on, in order that regular exception reports on items requiring action would be available. The company arranged for every supplier to be approached so as to establish realistic delivery times for every item.

It was decided to alter the materials purchasing policy and to procure items on a minimum/maximum stockholding principle. A minimum quantity level was set for each item in each store. This was the quantity level against which the combined totals of stock and on-order were measured for determining when to reorder. Similarly, a maximum quantity level was set for each item. An urge level was also set for each item in each store at a percentage of the minimum level, to enable progress action to be taken before stock runs out.

Every three months, the company gets a computer print out showing usage of each item for each of the previous three months and for the three quarters preceding that. Actual usage is compared with estimated usage. As all control levels — the minimum, maximum and urge — are based on usage and lead time, this information enables stock controllers to adjust control levels where necesary. Obsolete or slow moving items can also be identified (see Figure 7:1).

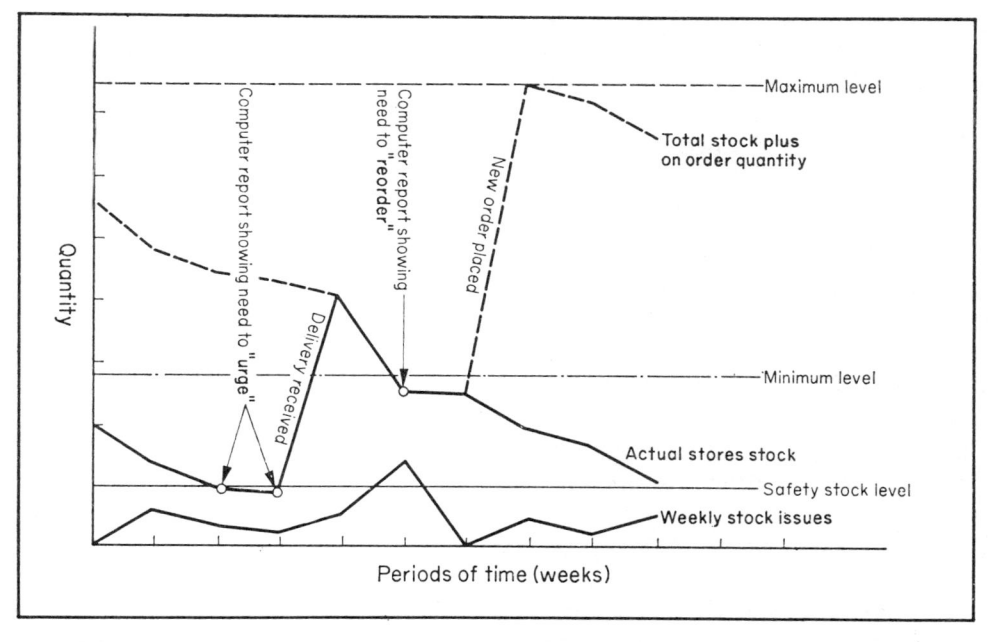

FIGURE 7:1   STOCK MOVEMENT AND LEVELS CONTROL, H W WARD

STOCK CONTROL SYSTEMS AND RECORDS

The total lead time is calculated by adding three figures:

1 The time allowed to raise the order and, where applicable, that to be allowed for insertion of job in forward load capacity
2 the manufacturing period for each item or else the delivery time by the outside supplier
3 the safety stock to safeguard against fluctuations in demand and late delivery or orders.

The average weekly usage and the total lead time having been determined for each item, the three levels can then be calculated. The minimum level is the average weekly usage figure multiplied by the total lead time in weeks. Urge level is a straight percentage of the minimum level. The maximum level is the average weekly usage quantity multiplied by the number of weeks allowed between reordering, and the result added to the minimum level quantity. This time allowance between reordering may vary from product to product or stores to stores, or whether the item is manufactured or purchased, but is usually in conformity with the company's policy on stock turn.

A monthly report is issued showing a complete valuation of stock in each stores and by product group, to provide management with financial holding figures and to show the rise or fall against previously set targets. This report also indicates excess holdings which can be offered for resale or to the works as an alternative to a more popular fast-moving line, where over-size material, for example, may be employed. It states:

- the value of stockholding in each store
- how much is on order
- how much has been issued during the month
- how much has been received during the month.

The report divides items by groups and details the items where excess stock exceeds a predetermined financial value.

Reordering

Every week, a tabulation is printed by the computer of items which require reordering, together with the week of delivery (see Figure 7:2). This is used both to originate purchase orders and to chase orders due or overdue for delivery. When an order is urged, this is noted on the file with the number of the week urged. Only items which require action are printed, but there is a

MANUFACTURING PROCESSES

facility to include any item desired by the stock controller to ascertain his stock, for example, or to assess his position for design change.

At the same time, transactions which could not be processed by the computer because of some error made by the storekeepers are tabulated, so that they may be reinserted the following week. A usual error is the misquotation of an item number or store.

The company gets from the computer twelve copies of its weekly report, which are distributed to the following:

1 the stock controller
2 purchasing, for progressing
3 store keepers
4 EDP department
5 commercial office—for staff to check before spares are promised
   to customers.

A price review tabulation is printed yearly to serve as the purchasing department's guide to where to purchase, the economic quantity to purchase and price to pay (see Figure 7:3). Amendments to the price review file are originated by the purchasing department when the invoiced price of newly received materials varies from the price on the order.

Coding

H W Ward uses a ten-digit code number for all stock items and assembly components.

The first digit denotes whether the item is manufactured or bought out of raw material. The next two digits indicate the material specification. The next four digits denote shape, finish and colour. The last three digits indicate the size of the item in thirty-seconds of an inch, so that 020, for instance, is equivalent to five-eighths of an inch. Such codes obviate duplication and allow new items to be inserted in the proper sequence.

The units of measure for each item have been standardised. Steel bars are charged by weight, but H W Ward buy and stock them by length. The price review print-out shows the price per foot even though the item is paid for by weight. One letter is sufficient — for example, *F* for feet and *P* for pounds.

Three letters denote location, even for every machine on the shopfloor, for use on the production planning sheets.

The first letter *W* denotes Worcester. The two others may refer to a store, when the second letter will be *Z*, and the third letter identifies the specific stores. For example, *WLM* means the light machine shop at Worcester. *WZA* denotes a specific store at Worcester.

The means of replenishing the stock is shown by four letters, as follows:

POSD means replenishing stocks by raising a purchase order on an outside supplier for a single (one time) delivery

MOOW means replenishing stocks by raising an internal manufacturing order on works

TWZA means replenishing stocks by indenting for transfer of materials from another stores (in this case stores WZA).

Each supplier is given a codeword of two letters followed by three numerals.

COLT INTERNATIONAL

Colt International, formerly Colt Heating and Ventilation Limited, is, as the name suggests, in the business of manufacturing heating and ventilation equipment mainly for industrial use.

Physical arrangement

Colt International moved to its present premises at Havant, Hants, in 1963, and all company activities have since been concentrated there. The factory area can be roughly divided into three sections, component manufacture, component stores and assembly area. The raw material feeds into the factory at one end of the component manufacturing bay. All material is delivered by lorries which reverse into a below-floor-level bay in the building and are unloaded by an overhead crane.

Adjacent to the press shop is the press tool stores, where over 1000 different tools are available. From these it is possible to produce components for any unit manufactured by the company during its existence.

The large stores are positioned between the manufacturing and assembly areas. Many component parts, and even subassemblies, are stored in this area, according to experience at a minimum stock level. On falling to this minimum stock level a note is issued to the manufacturing areas concerned to bring the stock of each part up to a safe working level.

In the assembly bay each regular model produced by the company has been isolated to its own section. According to the dispatch order, component parts are drawn from the central stores and delivered to the appropriate assembly area. The units are then built up in a series of jig fixtures secured to in-line benches.

Stock reorder and progress tabulation — Period 14

Reference	Stores	Replenishment source	UD	Maximum	Minimum	Urge	EOQ	Stock	On order	Delivery required	Order number	Date	Comments
1.16.1021.010	WZB	POMD	N	320	160	32	200	148	0	44	TW03276		Reorder
1.16.1021.030	WZB	POMD	N	480	240	48	300	141	75	46	N03987		Reorder
1.16.1021.035	WZB	POMD	N	480	240	48	300	73	100	46	N07697		Reorder
1.16.1021.060	WZF	TWZB	N	0	1—	1—	0	0	0				
1.16.1024.104	WZB	POMD	N	1600	800	400	1000	311	1984		AW00237	*Urge	
1.16.1024.104	WZF	TWZB	N	216	144	29	72	421	10		N05338		
1.16.1024.600	WZB	POMD	N	1600	800	400	1000	390	2000		AW00237	*Urge	
1.16.1025.100	WZB	POMD	N	112	56	12	60	6	93		AS00188	*Urge	
1.16.1025.100	WZF	POSD	N	0	1—	1—	0	6	0				
1.16.1029.116	WZB	POMD	N	1260	480	96	600	78	650		AW00237	Urge	
1.16.1029.116	WZB	POQD	N	320	160	32	200	17	235		N08060	Urge	
1.16.1035.100	WZB	POMD	N	640	320	64	400	31	400		AW00064	*Urge	
1.16.1039.020	WZB	POMD	N	960	480	96	600	261	165	46	N07697		Reorder

FIGURE 7:2 WEEKLY REORDER TABULATION, H W WARD

Price Review Listing

Reference number	S C F R X T	Supplier	U M	Unit of order	Conversion order—measure	Unit of price	Conversion price—measure	Price gross —unit price	Discounts % (1) (2) (3) (4)	Price net —unit price	Unit measure price	Date amended
1.28.1222.116	A*	CR200	N	NUM	1	NUM	1	3.74	20.00—	2.99	2.99	20/07/67
1.28.1223.167	A*	CR200	N	NUM	1	NUM	1	3.74	20.00—	2.99	2.99	18/04/67
1.28.1231.048	A*	CR200	N	NUM	1	NUM	1	3.32	20.00—	2.66	2.66	20/07/67
1.28.1231.050	A*	CR200	N	NUM	1	NUM	1	3.32	20.00—	2.66	2.66	18/04/67
1.28.1241.006	A*	CR200	N	NUM	1	NUM	1	1.24	20.00—	0.99	0.99	18/04/67
1.28.1241.008	A* Amendment 1	CR200	N	NUM	1	NUM	1	1.24	20.00—	0.99	0.99	18/04/67
	2							1.24	20.00—			02/10/67
	* 3	CR200	N	NUM	1	NUM	1	1.24	20.00—	0.99	0.99	02/10/67

FIGURE 7:3 PRICE REVIEW LISTING, H W WARD

STOCK CONTROL SYSTEMS AND RECORDS

Organisation

Stock control is the responsibility of the production controller, who is in turn responsible to the works director. In stock control proper, there are eight people, but others are involved who are responsible for seeing that the orders go out and for work scheduling. Stock control operates almost at the command of the product sections because only the product controller can say how the pattern of work is going.

The purchasing manager is also responsible to the works director, so that both he and the production control manager are colleagues and work together but neither is responsible to the other. Production control tells purchasing what to buy, when to buy and how much to buy. The only deviation from that is when purchasing can obtain a price advantage, because it, too, has a requirement to reduce costs over the year. So that if it can obtain a substantial cost reduction by ordering in bulk or delaying orders or bringing forward orders, it has the right to do so, providing production control can take responsibility for the items in stores.

Production control is not responsible for the warehouse of finished products. Although a large proportion of Colt products are manufactured to customer order, products are also manufactured for stock. As sales of heating and ventilating equipment fluctuate drastically in winter and summer, the stock helps to even out production over the year.

Stockholding

The company had at one time an extraordinarily low inventory and, while money was being saved from being tied up, there were critical shortages. Since then, the company has changed the formula on which stock level is calculated, and stock levels as a matter of policy have increased, so that the value of stockholdings has gone up considerably.

Operating routines

All parts are drawn by requisitions which are recorded on the bin and on the stock card. Units are broken down into parts and ordered partly by forecast and partly by usage.

About 7500 different items are stocked for production, ranging from nuts and bolts to expensive assemblies. The stock turnover aimed for is between four and five times a year, but varies according to the type of stock and seasonal fluctuations.

A physical inventory is taken once a year, but there is a running stocktaking every week by an auditor who is not responsible to production control He compares the actual quantity with the stated quantity and publishes a report every month showing discrepancies. Generally speaking, the error is extremely low. Discrepencies are simply made up; there is no investigation of them. Pilferage is very low.

Computerisation

The company used a consultant to help to analyse its production control methods. The first stage was to improve existing manual routines, and to devise a data processing scheme. It was decided to use a computer program:

1   to 'explode' monthly sales forecast and production programmes to identify requirements of
- (*a*) piece parts
- (*b*) labour
- (*c*) plant
- (*d*) material

2   to schedule purchases or bought out parts
3   to allocate customer orders against the planned production programme
4   to 'explode' customers' orders to requisitions and to final assembly instructions.

Investigations showed that the company would also be in a position to:

1   provide bought out parts and warehouse evaluation
2   eliminate stock record cards
3   value incoming raw materials from goods received notes, in total, month by month, for work in progress calculation
4   provide 'used on' lists for each part or assembly
5   compare dispatches by product with programme each month
6   produce schedule of parts, including amendments or modifications
7   identify slow-moving stock items
8   highlight planned made on works orders by prime work centres
9   produce made on works orders 'multi-item requisitions' and 'job completed' notifications
10   list unplanned issues of any parts
11   show excess stock held in terms of cover period against current programme.

STOCK CONTROL SYSTEMS AND RECORDS

Stock master

This file holds a record of each part and contains information regarding stock works orders, requirements etc. All stock movements, progress information and customers' orders are input daily. Amendments to data held on the master file, for example, product structure changes, are made weekly. Changes to the production programme as a result of monthly forecast meetings are made monthly.

Goods received notes are used to update the stock records when bought out parts are received from suppliers. Sub-contract items are treated as bought-out items, but in the case of items for which only certain operations are subject to sub-contract, *GRNs* are not recorded. *GRNs* from sub-contractors are ignored. These forms originate from and are completed in the stores sections (goods inwards). About fifty or sixty *GRNs* are received daily and contain:

1. the part number
2. quantity
3. date received.

The *GRNs* are batched for processing.

Material requisition

This document authorises the transfer of material from stock to work in progress. It is printed by the computer, attached to the finished works order and sent to the shopfloor by way of production control. It incorporates a part issue slip. When the material is actually issued, the stores foreman completes the reported start date and quantity issued. About 100 slips are returned each day to data processing.

Production programme

This document is used to input three months' production plans. At the initiation of this system, six-to-twelve months' production plans are fed in to set up the order and requirements pattern. After this point, three months' production plans are added quarterly. The production programme is completed by production control using forecasts supplied by marketing.

Reorder quantities

For made on works items, the computer bases order size on lead time, size of requirements, and batching rules set for each part individually. These take

MANUFACTURING PROCESSES

into account size of item and optimum batch sizes. For bought out items the purchasing department places orders from requirements batched in monthly totals by the computer. Certain items are identified as requiring special attention as regards cost, either because the supplier is unreliable or because it may be difficult for him to accelerate or decelerate when required.

A facility exists for establishing a safety stock on each and every part based on the unpredictability of the requirements of a part. If it is a made-in part it is fairly easy to calculate a buffer stock in terms of time and usage. Buffer stocks for bought out parts are based on supplier's lead time and how quickly he can deliver an urgently needed quantity.

Suppliers are given bulk orders and items are called off at predetermined rates. There is no consignment stock on the plant's site, but Colt are allowed extended credit by certain of their suppliers irrespective of when the goods are sold, which is preferred by the company to consignment stock.

The computer program does not progress actual purchase orders issued. To do this would need input of a great deal of information on orders, which would make more work than that occasioned by the purchasing routines used at present. However, the program identifies where — because of a change of programme or because sales have exceeded forecast — the requirement of a bought out part is changed. This changed requirement is interpreted by production control before passing new instructions, if required, to the purchasing departments. To be able to make these judgements, the production control department requires frequent and reliable information from purchasing on what orders have been placed.

Benefits

Since introducing the computer system the company has experienced the following benefits:

1 a one time reduction in stock level
2 stabilisation of staff level, and level of departmental performance maintained more economically, even under the strain of peak seasonal demand
3 earlier signalling of shortages by allocating all parts against customers' orders anticipated.

FORD MOTOR COMPANY LIMITED

The Ford Motor Company in the United Kingdom has integrated all those activities that have anything to do with the control of parts and materials and has made manufacturing, through its production planning and control organisation, autonomous for material flow.

The central staff of the production planning and control organisation is situated at the company's United Kingdom headquarters at Warley, Brentwood, Essex. Major company policies, objectives, plans and programmes relating to production planning and control are determined there and assistance and advice given the manufacturing groups on the techniques and systems which are implemented as far as possible uniformly in each of the seventeen plants in the United Kingdom.

The structure of production planning and control organisation differs slightly at each Ford plant and from that which exists at the central office. A typical layout of the production planning and control organisation may be seen in Figure 7:4.

Inventory

A stock of some 90 000 different parts, counting assembly units received as single parts, is maintained at Ford. This ranges from parts which are used at the rate of 2000 a day to those used only once a month. The usage rates change considerably and frequently according to fluctuating customers' requirements and the incorporation of engineering changes.

Inventory for Ford totals £200 million, not including materials which the company is legally or morally committed to accept from suppliers. In a typical plant, production planning and control manage about 40 000 different production and non-production parts, of which 30 000 are procured from outside the company. Daily usage is about 9 million parts, valued at about £6 million. The ratio of stock to sales is 10:1. The stock turnover rate varies at different plants, but the average is about ten times a year. At the Dagenham assembly plant, there is a turnover rate of seven days.

Ford estimate that the cost of keeping an item in stock is about 20 per cent of its value, including the cost of space, insurance, material handling equipment and potential return on money tied up in stock.

Setting objectives

The stock control system at Ford was implemented as a result of a comprehensive study, made in 1964, of engineering, manufacturing and sales. This study noted that the systems then in operation were complex and responded to change in requirements only with a great deal of effort and a long delay. The following recommendations were made:

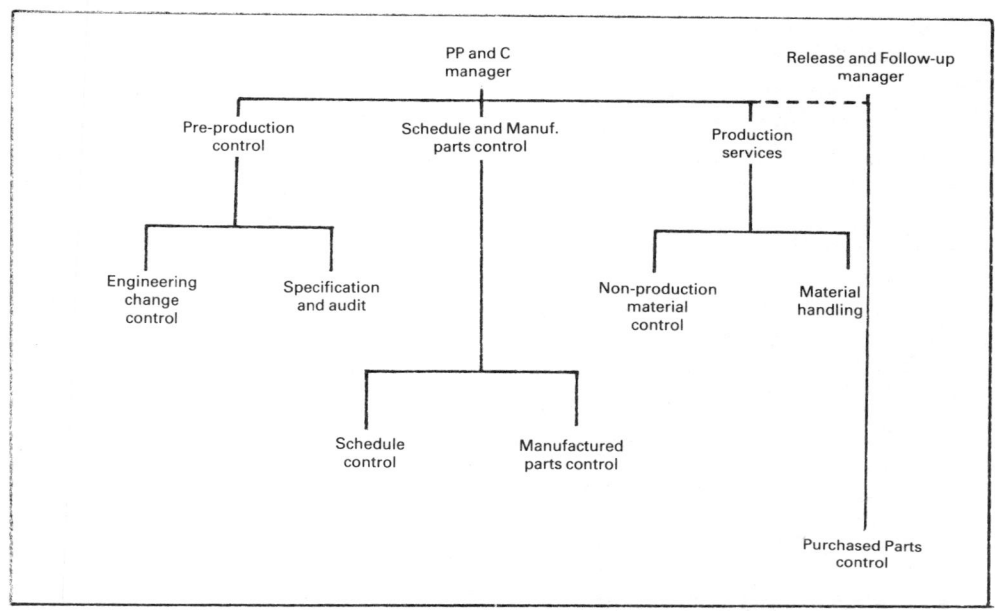

FIGURE 7:4 TYPICAL STRUCTURE OF PRODUCT PLANNING AND CONTROL, FORD

1   that first priority be given to converting product design through parts usage information to parts requirements and inventory control, as being the most important single feature requiring attention.
2   that information requirements within the company be handled through the establishment of fourteen master data files; these files to consist of:
 (a) a vehicle status file
 (b) a production parts master file controlling material flow and plant inventories
 (c) a pre-production parts master file catering for prototype engineering information
 (d) a facilities file to include machines and fixed assets
 (e) a manpower file to contain employee statistics and employee performance
 (f) a non-production parts master file containing information on indirect material, *and*
 (g) a parts supply operations master file, to be the basis of the supply of spare parts and various support files, such as dealer control, name and address and history.

STOCK CONTROL SYSTEMS AND RECORDS

The recommendations were accepted and a material control system was developed. The first segment deals with the forecasting of vehicle orders and the breaking down or 'explosion' of this forecast to parts. The second segment deals with the monitoring of vehicle orders against the original sales forecasting and the breakdown of vehicle to parts at the various stages of manufacture.

Scheduling

The third segment is the control of parts and part movements within manufacturing plants, the calculation of stock balances and their inventory value and the valuation of all movements of materials. The fourth segment allows for a management information retrieval system to provide information in a variety

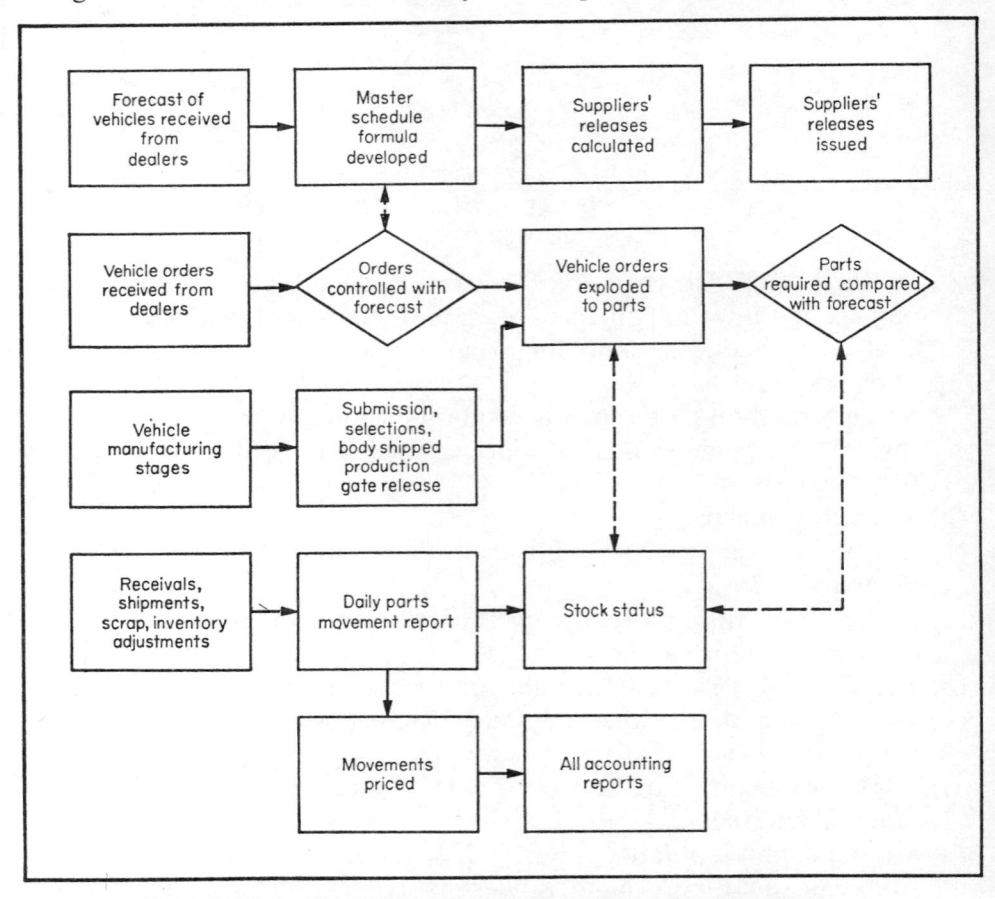

FIGURE 7:5 MATERIAL INFORMATION SYSTEM, FORD

of formats by exception or detail according to the requirements, and the fifth segment is the development of a data bank for pure accounting purposes. Each month the programming committee meet to:

1. ensure that capacities authorised are available in the plants
2. confirm that sales are selling the vehicles which have been built in line with the procurement programme
3. produce a six-month forecast broken down by features.

This data is then fed in the assembly releasing system, which is described later, and this calculates the 'call-in' of material from suppliers and produces the appropriate documentation at the same item as it forms the basis for scheduling the manufacturing plants.

Figure 7:5 outlines the flow of data affecting material flow at Ford.

The material control system was designed and supported entirely by the company. The file is designed rather like a Meccano set. If a part is bought from a supplier, room on the file is allocated for this one supplier. If a part is bought from three suppliers, space for three suppliers is allocated. Similarly, if a part is used in 100 engine types, 100 engine part numbers are shown as having a next-assembly relationship to this part. Up to a maximum of 20 000 characters of information may be carried for each part, but, on average, approximately 1500 are required.

Establishing controls

Each day, about 20 000 parts movements are processed. These include: receipts, shipments, scrap, inventory, adjustments and parts used directly in vehicles and 'knock downs' (vehicles to be assembled overseas). Control of materials intended for production — that is — items intended to become part of the completed vehicle, comprises different approaches:

1. features coding
2. a time advanced mechanism known as a 'float' *and*
3. cumulative records.

These three approaches apply to more than 80 per cent of the company's stock items. Everything else is considered to be fringe.

Production is planned by estimating future customers' orders and obtaining component parts in line with these estimates, and establishing a fluctuating stock level and lead time for each part required.

The customer indicates each particular characteristic wanted — model, engine capacity, left-hand or right-hand drive down to each small option — by ticking boxes on the order form. When these orders are received by the company, an entry value based upon a code structure is inserted against each feature and identifies the parts and material required. These details are then converted to punched cards and from these on to tapes to get the cumulative figure for each characteristic and 'explode' them into parts requirements for each month's production.

This scheduling system obviates the use of an assembly breakdown whereby each finished product is given an assembly number with a structure of subassembly and breakdown or parts and materials. The next assembly relationship is difficult to maintain, whereas the features or characteristics of a product remain much more static and require fewer relationships to maintain.

The manufacture of motor cars being a complex example, that of dolls provides a simpler illustration of the principle.

If, say, both black and white are produced, two characteristics have already been determined. The dolls may also have other permutations and combinations — male or female; black, blonde, or ginger hair; and perhaps blue, brown or hazel eyes. If the parts and materials in this example are related to the finished product, these multiply. If, however, the parts and materials are related to the characteristics which control their usage, there are fewer relationships to maintain. Black and white will control the pigments for plastic, for example, and that is really all that is needed to be known; there is no need to confuse it with the colour of eyes which has nothing to do with pigment.

In this example, if the parts and materials are related to finished product, there are thirty-six relationships to maintain, whereas if they are related to characteristics, they are simply added.

BODY COLOUR		
white or black	2	2
SEX		
male or female	$\times 2 = 4$	2
HAIR COLOUR		
black, blonde or ginger	$\times 3 = 12$	3
EYE COLOUR		
blue, brown or hazel	$\times 3 = 36$	3
		10

In the production of motor vehicles, millions of relationships have to be maintained on the next-assembly principle, whereas using characteristics as scheduling media across the whole product range produced by Ford, the

MANUFACTURING PROCESSES

company now needs to maintain only between 6000 and 7000 relationships as a result of its features coding. Issuing schedules on this basis would mean that all the material is scheduled to the end of the final assembly line, but of course a time advance is necessary to allow for previous processing, and safety banks of stock need to be created in the material flow to allow for contingencies and the differences between forecast and actual customer requirements.

Floats

It is not sufficient to provide just enough stock to supply the production line. Stock of material must be allowed to cover delays in the supply of parts to the line, transit from the supplier, processing, etc. Parts must therefore be obtained in advance of when they are scheduled to be used. This time advance at Ford is called a float. A float has five components:

1. *transit time:* the length of time between dispatch from a supplier or supply plant to receipt
2. *receiving/manufacturing frequency allowance:* the number of days' material required to maintain production from the first working day of each month to day of first receipt or manufacturing cycle
3. *operational reserve:* the ideal minimum number of days' material to be maintained in the receiving plant ahead of the first using operation
4. *system:* the number of days' material in use on the machine or assembly line
5. *shipping bank:* the ideal number of days' material held at the end of the production or assembly process.

Floats at Ford are always expressed in terms of days and not in terms of quantity. If, for instance, 1000 parts are on stock, this represents, at a current rate of usage of 500 a day, two days' stock.

In order that emphasis is placed on the parts according to daily usage value, each float is costed by accounts and is used for determining budget inventory levels against which actual inventory performance is controlled. A copy of each float calculation is sent to manufacturing engineering, which then has to establish space requirements and develop the layout of storage areas, and even determine the type of materials handling equipment required.

STOCK CONTROL SYSTEMS AND RECORDS

Cumulative records

Cumulative records are used by each Ford plant in the United Kingdom. It used to be found extremely difficult to control stocks, and these could not, in fact, be judged to be arithmetically correct unless cycle counters in each location synchronised their watches for simultaneous stock checks through their receiving areas, line feed and conveyor systems.

Inventory is now calculated simply by taking the cumulative value of materials in complete products going out from each manufacturing location and subtracting it from cumulative receipts of stock.

Ford are strong believers in establishing a datum point for all performance and concentrating management interest on exceptions from the established standards. If, for instance, the daily production report states that 999 out of the 1000 vehicles scheduled for production have been completed, what management concerns itself with is the one vehicle not produced as planned. This principle of managment by exception permeates all management functions at Ford, including stock control.

Operational procedures

Production planning and control at Ford is making increasing use of computers for:

1. recording and tabulating stock movements.
2. calculating requirements for component parts and producing a schedule for the supplier
3. vehicle scheduling
4. tabulating scrap, etc.
5. recording production counts of own manufactured parts.

The major programme for all production materials is run on an IBM 370/158 and tapes are processed at group headquarters at Warley, which is responsible for coding, sifting and sorting all information to produce requirements for each location. It took Ford five years to consolidate its present computer system. The company devised its own program and wrote its own systems specifications and it makes its own systems analysis of production materials. Non-production materials are not yet controlled by computer.

What is called stock control in other firms can be subdivided into three separate functions at Ford:

1. schedule control

MANUFACTURING PROCESSES

2   parts control *and*
3   vehicle scheduling

Schedule control. The schedule control activity produces an overall company schedule from which requirements of all parts can be calculated, whether bought outside the company or made in Ford plants. Ford plants schedule about 3000 vehicles a day, using about 3000 items each, giving them a daily usage of about 9 million items valued at approximately £6 million. In the assembly plants there are ten days' worth of orders at all times and these are topped up daily to replace those used in each day's production. The number and type of orders submitted are measured against what should have been submitted against the forecast; this is known as order submission control.

One problem is the difference between sales forecasts and actual requirements, which can lead to either shortages or surpluses. The company has tried the most sophisticated techniques in forecasting, but has invariably returned to the judgement of experienced individuals and major customers who know the markets.

Through the feature coding on specification sheets the parts analyst can identify slow-moving or obsolete items. As usage is reduced, stockholding is revised, until it gets to the point where the item is discontinued. All these parts come out on a separate listing of run down stock.

While the computer is calculating the stock balance, the part movements are valued at standard and actual prices and the information is recorded on a history file. This file is assessed daily, weekly and monthly, to produce a variety of cost control reports, the most important of which is the 'computed packing slip', a sort of priced advice note. This document is matched against the production material invoice and has eliminated the comparing of invoices with purchase orders and comptometer checking invoice extensions on about 70 per cent of all invoices controlled on this system. The other 30 per cent are in discrepancy and require manual handling.

The 230 men working in purchased parts control are divided by types of commodities for which they are responsible and are grouped so that only one man deals with a supplier whenever possible. Each man advises suppliers, by means of a 'release', the quantity required of each item, when and where the next month's deliveries are to be made, and also the forecast requirements for the subsequent five months, so that the supplier may plan his production (see Figure 7:6). This is, generally, not a company commitment for the latter months. The parts analyst is also responsible for ensuring that the parts are delivered according to the instructions given on the monthly release. He can also authorise suppliers to pull ahead of schedule when alternative suppliers of

Ford Motor Company Limited

Release Authorisation — Abruf für Produktionsmaterial

3A 097764

Firma Abex Pagid Reibbelag G
Postfach 58
4300 Essen Bergehreck
W.Germany

Progr. Nr.	Date/Datum	U.M. M.E.	Partname/Teilbezeichnung		Partnumber/Teilnummer	Fin. C.
378-2	29.06.83	01	9055044-KIT-PAD FRNT BRAKE	H77FG	2K021AA	

Ship to Plant/Anlieferwerk	Rec. Location/Abladestelle	Parts Analyst/Materialdisponent	Book/Buch
AVELEY R/S	DEXINE		0210

Fabrication Auth./Fabrikation Freig.

Material Auth./Material Freig.

NOTE ANNUAL HOLIDAY 1983.24 JULY 1983-3 WEEKS-14 AUGUST 1983

Last Shipment considered/Letzte erf. Lieferung

Document Ref./Lieferschein Nr.

Date/Datum Quantity/Menge Cumulative Endzahl +/- Last Rel/Bedarfsänderung	Immediate/Sofort										

Continued/Fortsetzung

Date/Datum Quantity/Menge Cumulative Endzahl +/- Last Rel/Bedarfsänderung											

Date/Datum	30.06	7.07	14.07	21.07	28.07	31.07	31.08	30.09	31.10	30.11	31.12	
Working Days/Arbeitstage	22.0	5.0	5.0	5.0	0.0	0.0	13.0	21.0	22.0	22.0	16.0	

SUB TOTAL

ADJ.DETAILS ST.INV. SCRAP SCRAP% % MIS.DIS 25 INVAD J 1.ADJ% % REL.ADJ 200

SVO PRD KD MPO ENG.DEV FREQ CD ERRORS E1

Mat Plan Aug 1978 EU 3086

MDH77FG 2K021AA

1 2 3 4 5 6 7 8 9 10 11 12 13 14 15 16 17 18 19 20 21 22 23 24 25 26 27 28 29 30 31

FIGURE 7:6 RELEASE AUTHORISATION, FORD

the same parts are unable to meet schedule commitments or when actual production requirements deviate from schedule.

In order to convert customers' orders into requirements of parts and assemblies, a scheduling formula index of code numbers is compiled by the schedule formula activity. Each code number is allocated in such a way that groups of parts which are dependent upon particular features (but not necessarily related physically) may be identified by code numbers. While there are millions of derivatives in the Ford range of products, each complete model range can be identified by about 2000 SFI codes. The SFI codes are used to specify usage and requirement data in a condensed form in collating schedules and in reporting orders submitted and production achieved.

The parts control analysts receive a daily exception report known as the critical shortage report. This report lists all the parts that are in 'critical' shortage condition according to predetermined parameters. The analyst takes appropriate action to ensure that further supplies will be available to ensure continuity of production. On the date receipt of goods is expected, a parts control man will ring the supplier and first of all, reach agreement on the cumulative total of receipts of each item since 1 January each year. He then checks that the goods have been dispatched. Where troublesome items or suppliers are concerned, the parts control man will establish the route by which the material is being delivered and the number of the vehicle; he will ring the supplier again if the goods are not received in the time estimated.

A physical spot check is made on quantities of items received, particularly those which show a continuous discrepancy in stock level, by matching advice note and invoice. Suppliers are usually honest and more often send more goods not less than are stated on the advice note and invoice. Suppliers are generally responsible for maintaining quality and Ford carries out its own quality check on goods received. An asterisk is placed against suppliers that are quality assured; that is, those who have quality controls that have fully satisfied Ford inspectors.

All goods received by 1600 each day are posted on record, and cumulative reports are issued at 08 30 the next day on a stock status report from the computer (see Figure 7:7). The stock status report shows the quantity of each part on hand that day and indicates the stock status in relation to the forthcoming vehicle orders in the plant for the next four days and current month's requirement. Each man gets his own copy containing the parts for which he is responsible, where used, the float, and the present inventory balance which gives him an actual stock status at that point in time. In addition, each analyst gets a copy of the daily transaction register for his parts which details all stock movements that have occurred the previous day — re-

0719A/28

STOCK RATIOS FOR THE PERIOD ENDING 31.3.83

Stock ratios are calculated by dividing the net value of issues by the average of COSMOS stock valuations at close-down periods

				31.8.82	31.12.82	31.3.83	31.8.82	31.12.82	31.3.83	Minimum desired ratio	Target ratio
350	HA	Batteries	)	185	279	388	2.39	2.62	2.38	3.00	4.00
	JA	Electrical	)	72,740	64,610	65,923					
351	G	Science		96,387	65,173	75,400	2.60	3.21	3.03	3.00	4.00
	HG	Cleaning HCL	)	172	248	129					
	Z	Alcohols		4,184	4,185	5,335	9.32	6.46	5.94	4.00	4.50
352	Q	Timber		64,466	75,920	63,576	5.82	5.02	5.96	5.00	6.00
353	O	Furniture		242	572	2,850	1.99	3.02	2.21	-	-
354	HL	Cleaning Aids	)	12,508	10,262	11,535	3.68	4.15	3.58	3.40	4.00
	L	Holloware/ Crock	))	175,564	161,1924	202,512					
355	HB	Turps/Sand	)	6,630	2,281	7,278	4.19	4.14	3.78	3.50	4.00
	JB	Ironmongery	)	74,789	82,170	73,642					
	N	Sanitaryware	)	25,416	37,008	59,954					
	PB	Inflammables	)	2,417	2,419	2,138					
356	GD	Horticulture		4,246	1,636	36	2.71	5.83	5.88	4.00	4.50
	HJ	Oils		217	256	117	2.60	2.46	3.11	3.00	4.00
	J	Tools & Engin	)	91,225	84,582	87,347					
	NJ	Anvils		531	382	454					
	P	Inflammables	)	814	704	665					
	TJ	Top Engin	)	1,584	1,158	1,649					
358	JJ	AVA		-	17,856	17,940	-	9.79	7.33	-	-
451	GH	Cleaning Misc	)	832	783	474	10.14	8.07	8.12	10.00	12.00
	HT	Top Cleaning	)	125,394	113,117	139,386					
	H	Textiles & Cleaning	))	96,491	72,264	97,292	5.54	5.30	4.98	5.50	5.50
	K	Sheeting/ Ropes	))	1,362	825	1,513					
	MH	LFB Bed Linen	)	1,211	1,881	2,610	14.36	7.99	9.31	14.00	16.00
	GX	Medical		68,133	44,579	55,360	4.54	5.05	4.80	5.00	6.00
	HX	Top X		5,367	2,602	3,944					
	LH	Hollo/Cleaning	)	-	946	577					
452	E	Floor Coverings	))	45,322	31,210	37,171	3.96	3.82	5.41	4.00	5.00
453	C	Civilian Clothing	))	30,913	30,309	37,357	3.37	4.17	2.99	3.00	4.00
	HF	Household Gloves	))	11,568	6,169	22,217					
	M	Uniform Clothing		262,857	298,838	228,971	3.14	3.66	4.75	2.60	4.00
	MF	Footwear		66,107	55,974	73,619	2.68	3.76	2.97	2.50	3.00
457	HW	Cleaning Lamps	))	980	1,442	827	13.39	7.31	10.98	5.50	6.00
	W	Lamps	)	44,737	100,747	54,795					
	JW	Misc Lamps	)	8,957	2,159	2,217					
459	V	Electrical DMES		39,350	38,932	35,130	1.81	1.37	1.34	3.00	4.00
551/3		Food		665,478	402,268	576,411	18.95	22.38	18.49	18.00	20.00

FIGURE 7:7 STOCK STATUS REPORT, FORD

MANUFACTURING PROCESSES

ceipts, usages, miscellaneous disbursements, scrap etc. The purpose of this report is to assist the analyst to monitor the movement of production material into stock status records, ensure that the supplier has delivered as planned, highlight any unexpected stock variances etc. It was designed with the intention of controlling parts to meet established inventory levels, maintain production in line with schedules, and bring about a reduction of stock.

C   critical stock level
L   low stock level
E   excess stock level.

Excess and inadequate stock levels must be adjusted separately in the next schedule. When it is foreseen that the normal calculated float for a part will be insufficient to cope with rising schedules, the existing float levels can be increased either permanently or for a temporary period.

Parts control. Production planning and control does not decide which items to hold in stock. The engineering release, specifying which items are required for production, is the authority for holding the items in stock. Having initiated that specification, it is then necessary to send a requisition for an item to purchasing.

All parts used in the production of vehicles are contained on the production parts master file. Each part is numbered. For each part held on the master file on which amendments have occurred, a parts control record is printed once a week consolidating the total amendments input during the preceding week. The information printed on the form is divided into two categories:

1   base record, the portion which is applicable to all parts held on the master file, *and*
2   variable record which may be applied to some parts and not to others.

The information on this form includes using and supplying plant, location in using plant, stock location, code part name, cost class, whether bought or made, date, part number, units of measure in which part is used and procured, status of part, commodity type, cycle check frequency, float, production rate, minimum shipment quantity, frequency of delivery, and other data intended for accounts or purchasing.

Vehicle scheduling. The scheduling system centres round a suite of program-

STOCK CONTROL SYSTEMS AND RECORDS

mes known collectively as the vehicle scheduling control record (*VSCR*) system. This is divided roughly into three major sections based on the three main files:

1   *the feasibility check table*, which analyses orders to ensure that values punched are feasible
2   *the SFI 'explosion' table*, which breaks down the feasible order to SFI code
3   *the vehicle master status file*, which includes an image of the order card, the SFI code 'explosion' of the order, and a status indicator with pertinent dates which are constantly updated.

As customers' orders do not arrive in a sequence which is ideal for production planning purposes, the vehicle scheduling system arranges the orders to satisfy both production operations and customers. Sales are notified daily of the quantity and types of vehicles to be submitted for production:

    15 days ahead for heavy commercial vehicles
    12 days ahead for light commercial vehicles
    10 days ahead for passenger vehicles.

Each order is translated into a computer punched card giving all relevant details, and the card is returned to sales, where it is filed.

If necessary, orders are shuffled to provide suitable mixes for manufacturing purposes. A computer document is produced showing:

1   the breakdown of orders by SFI codes
2   the day's submission schedule
3   the actual submissions for that day
4   the cumulative submissions month-to-date
5   the cumulative submissions year-to-date
6   the comparison between submissions and schedule.

Parts analysts then check the days' value of the orders to ensure that adequate stock is available to build the vehicle, using the exception principle. At a specified time before the actual production date (six days for commercial vehicles and four days ahead for passenger vehicles), the computer punched cards are extracted from the order bank to make up the necessary quantity and types of parts to meet the operating schedule for the build date. These cards are passed to computer operations, who produce:

MANUFACTURING PROCESSES

1   production record cards *and*
2   vehicle specification sheets.

The original cards are submitted to the computer for incorporation into the *VSCR*. This shows:

1   submissions selected year to date
2   the date when the finished vehicle is scheduled to come off the final line.

A production card accompanies the vehicle as it goes through assembly, giving a mechanical report of each process, to show, in effect, what did happen in production as opposed to what should have happened. Theoretically, it would be possible to pick up a card at any point in assembly and trace it back to the original source — that is, sales. The card is normally taken up at the shipping bay when the vehicle is completed to relieve production of the stock used.

The smooth flow of the system is frequently disrupted by labour disputes both at Ford and its suppliers. Strikes are a dreary and costly business, and nowhere is this more evident than in the motor industry. But Ford has a reputation for being the first to recover from a strike and the last to suffer the effects of one. Indeed, none of the supplier strikes in 1969 caused Ford workers to lose a single day's employment, though they caused a loss of 5 per cent of the year's production.

The company keeps comprehensive records of strikes at suppliers and each day prints a report containing details of the strike, its beginning and duration, parts affected, daily usage and number of days' stock available (see Figure 7:8).

Production schedules can be changed or different items be substituted. When Ford lost supplies of the metal seat frames for the Cortina de Luxe models early in 1970, production was kept going by putting a superior seat frame in, although this cost an extra £2 a car. The company also explores alternative sources, and the parts control manager keeps a record of each part, and the alternative sources and overseas Ford plants where the same part is locally procured. Knockdown parts for overseas delivery are also sometimes diverted, since they have a longer lead time for delivery and others can be sent by plane to fulfil delivery. It is not unknown for the company to obtain the parts required from dealers' shelves.

Ford **Highly Critical Shortages**

Special Allocation of Items

Purchased Parts ✓

Man...

Supplier (Vendor/Manufacturing Plant) Dai Farmer (Wales) Limited

Cause [illegible]

Supply Items (Type of Material) Crip pipes, Springs, Cruns

Date (Commenced) 11/5/83

Relevant Info: Union meeting 19/5/83

Alternative Source None

User Plant	Part Number	Description	Models Affected	Daily Usage	Stock as at: 0800 Plant	P.S.O.	K.D.	Re-work	Tran-sit			Stock runs through: 13/5 D	13/5 N	14/5 D	14/5 N	15/5 D	15/5 N	16/5 D	16/5 N	17/5 D	17/5 N	Promise
PTA Dag	1111 x 222224	Crip pipe	All	4000	16000																	
PTA Dag	22224 1111 x	Crun	All	2000	4000																	Trying to fly Germany

Air Freight

P.P.C. Nov 70 2788

FIGURE 7:8 CRITICAL SHORTAGE REPORT, FORD

MANUFACTURING PROCESSES

Future development

Ford has developed a mechanised inventory budget and performance monitoring system. A more sophisticated accounts-payable system has been proposed, which will link the automatic payment of invoices with receipt of materials.

PFIZER LIMITED

Pfizer Limited is the principal United Kingdom subsidiary of the worldwide Pfizer Organisation founded in New York in 1894. The company has, since 1945, grown into a multinational concern with an annual turnover in excess of £300 million, and with over eighty manufacturing plants in thirty-two countries. In Britain, Pfizer manufactures and markets a wide range of science-based products, including prescription medicines, chemicals, veterinary and animal health products, antiseptics, dietary aids, perfumes and cosmetics.

The Pfizer site at Sandwich, Kent, where the company has been established since 1953, houses extensive medicinal research laboratories and a large and versatile chemical manufacturing plant in which antibiotics, sysnthetic drugs, vaccines and organic acids are produced. A total of nearly 2000 persons is employed by the company at Sandwich. Of these approximately 400 are engaged in research. The company holds 16 500 items for production, in pure powder forms, bar raw materials and packaging, and including engineering spares and stationery. Finished products are the responsibility of the planning department, independent of stock control.

Staff

There are twenty-six people involved in stock control and storekeeping, including a stores foreman and three chargehands in each store, all working under the stock controller, who in turn is responsible to the production controller. In the stock control office are three clerks who look after stock control records, a typist and a filing clerk.

Stock control clerks are promoted from stores because the experience they have gained there enables them to appreciate the size of the components and the problems involved with different items.

Once a month, the stock controller and the three stock control clerks hold a three-hour seminar on a late Friday afternoon to discuss their working methods and to undertake further training. For example, they do exercises to calculate what quantity they would hold for certain items, and they then go into the stores to calculate the cost of holding those quantities.

STOCK CONTROL SYSTEMS AND RECORDS

Coding system

Until a few years ago, Pfizer had a rather sophisticated coding system for raw materials intended for production, but the company dispensed with it when it was thought to have become too complicated. The company started with a seven-digit system main classification and coded with a part number every item appertaining to a product until it eventually reached eighteen digits. An attempt was made to use the digits to group them by raw materials, packaging components and the way they were produced; and then to include the price and stock location (it was hoped eventually to include the source). The whole set up became unwieldy and, worse, the codes stopped having any significance to storemen and others on the shopfloor.

Pfizer decided to devise a simple system which would be easy to understand and enable people to identify quickly the correct item required. When the Pfizer plant at Folkestone was amalgamated with the Sandwich plant a few years ago, the opportunity was taken to do this when combining stock.

All items were grouped alphabetically under the names by which they were commonly known, as capsules, for example. Each item was then given a four-digit number with an alpha prefix to indicate the group. While the storeman used never to know the significance of long codes, he now knows, at least by the prefix, what type of item is being referred to:

LA raw material ordered from the UK
LB non-active blends
LR raw material (recovered) — identical code number to *LA* series
LX raw material ordered outside the UK
KA active material ordered and produced in the UK
KB active blends
KX active material ordered outside the UK
KZ finished goods (strip packing, etc)
RM return animal feeds.

LA — raw material ordered from the United Kingdom — includes supplies produced by Pfizer itself. The symbol *LX*, used to refer to imported raw materials, proved useful when the Government imposed a surchage on imports, since imported goods were easily identified.

LB refers to blend. In making certain products, different blends of ingredients must be mixed. When a blend is completed, a code is given to it.

LR covers everything returned from Pfizer productions units. For example, take *LA* 0001, which may have been issued to production. If 4000 gallons are left over, but it cannot be kept on the production floor or in stores, stock control takes it back under *LR* 0001.

MANUFACTURING PROCESSES

Any item with a *K* in the prefix means an active raw material. An 'active' is the basic ingredient which gives the product its potency. Penicillin, for instance, is an active material. An active is essential to the product and cannot be substituted. The distinction is also made to identify the most costly ingredients in purchasing and in production. *KB* refers to an active blend.

RM refers to animal feeds returned. There is an expiry date on animal feeds, as there is on anything pharmaceutical and agricultural. This means that expired goods cannot be sold over the counter to a customer after a specific date. Obviously, a merchant sends back goods due to expire shortly, and stock control must keep a check on what is returned and isolate it under a separate coding. These goods are treated as rejects.

Digits. Digits in the coding structure, as had been stated, signify nothing and new items are added sequentially. If an item becomes redundant, the code is re-used after six months, which gives accounts enough time to close all paper work dealing with any previous item with this code.

A different series of numbers is used for packaging components, such as cotton wool, elastic bands, etc. Anything that is a container, bottles, tin, polythene bags etc. goes under *PB*. *PC* means that an item is a packaging cap. (The company has recently standardised the size cap to fit many different bottles.)

Manuals

Stock catalogues of all items stocked are available for reference by those who have to draw materials from stores. Each manual gives the code number of the item, the description and the cost per unit in which it is purchased. Terminology has proved to be a problem, since items can be listed under several different headings.

The number of manuals issued varies according to the items included. For pharmaceutical packaging, for instance, there are only five copies — for stock control, stores, quality control, packaging technology and pharmaceutical production — and they include actual samples of cartons, labels, inserts etc. On the other hand, there are about 150 copies throughout the company of the stationery items and sundries manual.

A separate manual gives the finished products and their components, including packaging, so that in scheduling production it is easy to indicate how many component parts are needed. If, say, 20 000 of a product are going to be made, it is known that 20 000 plus standard coverage of each of the items listed in the manual under this product will be required.

STOCK CONTROL SYSTEMS AND RECORDS

These manuals have cut down on inquiries and have helped to reduce the variety of items from 18 500 to 16 500.

The computer is used for breakdowns of production programmes, as well as packaging programmes once weekly, monthly and bi-annually. The computer printout gives a complete tabulation of all items by code, by full description, by part number, by cost, and by usage. When actual stock held is needed quickly, to check whether or not a production change can be accommodated, for example, or to determine how the supply will be affected if a delivery is delayed, the appropriate record clerk checks his balance from his record card. This is quicker than programming the computer and waiting for results.

Engineering items apart, production raw materials are turned over every three weeks on average, some every twenty-four hours and some every six weeks. Packaging items are turned over monthly whenever possible. On overall production, there is a complete turnover about every four weeks.

Safety stock for products such as Diabenes is naturally very high. Safety stock for more ordinary products averages about a fortnight. How much finished stock to hold is an important decision, and here stock control works closely with distribution and planning.

Stocktaking

An annual inventory is taken by external auditors but stock control has a progressive stocktaking, covering so many items a day from beginning to end of the catalogue. Engineering stock is checked thoroughly every four months. The rest, pharmaceuticals, packaging, raw materials, active materials, stationery, are checked monthly.

Rate of issues from stores depends on the category an item belongs to. With the exception of engineering reserves, however, there is a complete turnover of stock on an average of every three or four weeks.

The planning department knows the maximum output that can be obtained for any given product on the production unit, and the production programme is planned according to this. The schedules are then turned over to stock control, where they are broken down into the number of components or raw materials needed to meet each batch.

The reorder level for items intended for production is really a safety level, and depends very much on the time of year and on the lead time. On engineering items and such items as stationery, the company works on a straight reorder level based on past usage.

Twice a year, stock control sends to user departments a list of items used and the quantity used in the previous six months, and the user departments are asked whether the usage will rise or fall and by how much. Invariably, they say the usage rate will rise. The predicted rise is then checked by the stock control department.

The stock controller is responsible for informing purchasing of what supplies are needed and the quantity.

Economic order quantity

Pfizer tries to calculate economic order quantities for stock items but is finding that most of its suppliers now insist on minimum order quantities, which are getting larger and larger. Suppliers dislike setting up production lines for small orders.

The company breaks down requirements for all items for the year and sends to each supplier an estimate of what it will be buying for the year. The supplier may get two orders a year or one order a month, say. For items used constantly, deliveries are arranged once monthly or every week, to keep inventories down. This method works well until suppliers, for one reason or another, are unable to deliver as scheduled. On certain items, the company has a moral and legal obligation to customers. It cannot afford to run out of Diabenes, a prescription for diabetics, for example. Products such as these are called A1 products. Very large reserve stocks are held on them, and in no circumstances will the company run out.

Pfizer constantly finds lead times for supplies increasing. The company used to be able to get supplies to its Sandwich plant from the Midlands in two or three days. Now, the average is five days. The buying office turn round orders every twenty-four hours, which is good, but this adds another two days to the lead time. Every supplier is asked to state the notice required for delivery. Some items have a twenty-six weeks' delivery lead time. Ten per cent is added to this as a reserve stock or reserve lead time, and this has proved adequate.

Stock control does not check quality of goods that arrive. Quality control gets a copy of the goods received note and checks all goods received which require technical inspection, such as fans and heaters.

Goods recorded on stock control cards are posted within half an hour of receipt or issue. This is achieved by grouping stock in order of priority, beginning with production items and ending with stationery and office supplies.

Small order system

Recently, stock control has started placing orders directly on suppliers, under a new system agreed to by the buying department.

STOCK CONTROL SYSTEMS AND RECORDS

A form is made out as a request to purchase, but can be utilised as a purchase order when authorised by the stock controller and the buyer (see Figure 7:9). There are five copies of the form: two go directly to the supplier, one copy to stores, one to stock control and the last to purchasing. The supplier keeps one copy as proof of order, and the other he sends in with the goods. In this way the company has done away with the requisition and buying office routines, and with the advice note and the goods received note. When the goods come in, the copy returned is married up by the storesman with the copy which was sent to him; he checks the material and signs the form. The top copy then becomes a goods received note and is passed to stock control for its records to be updated and to the buying office to await the invoice.

```
                    [Pfizer]
              Engineering stock order
Supplier                              Order number _____
                                      Date _____
```

Code number	Material description	Quantity ordered	Unit cost	Suppliers use – Quantity dispatched	Quantity received	Store use

Copies: White copy (2) Supplier
        Green copy (1) Buying office
        Pink copy (1) Stock control   Order approved
        Blue copy (1) Stores

Stock controller _____

Buying department _____

All queries to be addressed to stock control, [Pfizer Limited]

FIGURE 7:9 REQUISITION/PURCHASE ORDER FORM, PFIZER

MANUFACTURING PROCESSES

These buying orders are made out with as many as ten items on each of them and the system cuts down considerably on paper work and lead time. The system is not used for quality controlled materials. As, however, 75 per cent of items procured are engineering, sundries and stationery, which do not undergo quality control, the company is saving something in the region of 1000 buying orders, 1000 goods received notes, 1000 advice notes and 1000 request to order forms, not to mention the labour saved, reduced inventory and lead time.

The major problem is to get suppliers to agree to the system. To do this, each supplier is guaranteed a year's business by the company, on condition that he guarantees, in return, reliable delivery service, that he holds at his expense a month's stock at his warehouse, and that he is willing to use Pfizer forms. Each supplier is given a complete list of code numbers, description, the estimated annual requirement, and the usual call off size.

Dead stock — and new stock

Stock is reviewed every three or six months, according to the value, to isolate slow-moving or obsolete items. Slow-moving items are identified by going through the records and flagging any item that has not been used. After three months a list is made of these and sent to the originating department. The items are put up for disposal straight away with the agreement of the accounts department.

Any new item to be put in stock must be authorised by the production director, if it is a production item, or the chief engineer, if it is an engineering item. The request to place a new item in stock is made on a standard request form (see Figure 7:10 and 7:11). They also have to provide the name of suppliers, if known, and, if it is an engineering item, the part number, the cost and the estimated usage. As a general rule, goods must be used at the rate of at least one a month before being put in stock.

An exception is slow-moving engineering spares. A spare part to cover a plant breakdown may not be needed this year or the next, but when it is needed it will be needed immediately. What is the point of disposing of a piece of electrical or engineering spare which cost £150 and could take thirty-five weeks to replace if it is critical to the operating of a plant costing £4000 to £5000 a day? There would be no saving here.

Pfizer works on the assumption that if it cannot provide a finished item, somebody else will. Statisticians will have their theories, facts and figures, but it is impossible to assess the value of an item to the customer when he cannot obtain it. If a chemist cannot get a dependable supply from one supplier, he

STOCK CONTROL SYSTEMS AND RECORDS

	Request to place new materials on stock/or amendment	Serial number _____ for stock control use
To: <u>Stock control</u> Part A: To be completed by department		

Part A:
Department requesting:	
Full description of item:	
Supplier:	
Cost:	
Estimated annual usage:	
Usage per batch:	
Estimated first quarter requirement:	
Product material to be used in:	
Date new material required by:	
Special instructions:	_____ Departmental head Requesting new item:

Part B: To be completed by stock control

Code number	Description	R/order level	R/order quantity	Remarks

Stock control manager—Date   Production controller—Date   Pharmaceutical director—Date

This form is to be used to place new material on stock or amend existing stock items except the following:

A Raw materials used in products covered by the production programme are placed on stock by the new product record of ordering form taken from the manufacturing instructions

B Packaging materials used in the manufacturing departments are placed on stock by the approved packaging specification/new record of ordering form

C Engineering materials are placed on stock by the "request to place on stock authority engineering department" form

All other materials that are requested to be placed on stock are required to be covered by this form

Note:

1 Please complete Part A fully before the form is sent to stock control

2 Artwork, if required, is to accompany this form

3 Quotations are to be attached to this form wherever possible

4 Under the heading "special instructions"—if an amendment is required to a stationery item—layout—size, etc, details to be given in the "special instructions" column

FIGURE 7:10   NEW STOCK ITEM REQUEST FORM, PFIZER

To: Stock control manager [Pfizer Limited—Sandwich] Serial number

Application for additions to engineering stores stock

To be completed by engineering/project department

Part *A* — This material is required as spare for the following equipment

Description	Manufacturer
Plant number	Manufacturer's drawing number
Original contractor	Manufacturer's serial number
Original order number	Date of original order

Part *B* — New engineering stock items required

Item	Code number	Detailed description	Material	Part number or drawing number	Suggested minimum stock	Estimated usage per year	Price each	Vocabulary number	Date received

Engineering department initiator ______________ Date _________

Engineering department approved ______________ Date _________

Stock control authorised ________________ Date _________

FIGURE 7:11 APPLICATION FOR ADDITIONS TO ENGINEERING STORES STOCK, PFIZER

STOCK CONTROL SYSTEMS AND RECORDS

will go to another, who not only can provide hime with that item but a whole range of other products as well.

Every part has a location in the stores; each lane is numbered, each rack is numbered and each bin is numbered. There are bin location cards, but location does not appear on the catalogues.

Stock is divided into groups according to value. Previously, the company was taking as much time controlling sixpence worth of items as a £100 piece of equipment. All raw materials were classified according to the *ABC* principle and the stock controller was shocked to find that 5 per cent of the materials totalled 87 per cent of inventory value.

The most expensive materials at Pfizer are the 'actives'. These are stock checked every morning at 08 00 and again each evening at 17 00. Greater attention is also paid to certain items, such as imported material, which are more crucial to production than are other items, although they may not be more expensive.

For low-value items, nuts, bolts, washers, any item worth less than £0.25, in fact, the company works on a two-bin system. Five years ago this system had been rejected because it was not thought that proper control could be kept with it, but since its implementation, the system has proved to work quite well. If it is necessary to know exactly how many items are on hand at any one time, however, they must be counted.

The same system is applied to office stationery and sundries, and paper work has been cut by about 50 per cent in the area. The employee must still obtain such items from the stores counter, and needs authorisation from his superior for an unusually large amount of supplies. Copies of the signatures and initials of authorised persons are placed in each store.

In effect, there are controls but greatly reduced paper work, which should be the aim of any good stock control system.

Appendix

Checklist for Analysing Effectiveness of Stock Control System

1. What is the ratio of stock value to sales turnover?
2. What is the service level or fraction of demand immediately filled from stock?
3. What is the service level aimed at?
4. What other standards or measures are employed to assess efficiency of department?
5. How is slow-moving, surplus or unsaleable stock identified?
6. How much does it cost to carry an item in stock?
7. How is this figure arrived at?
8. What uses are made of it?
9. How is a new item added to the stock range?
10. What is the procedure for adding it to records?
11. How are the quantity and quality of goods delivered checked?
12. How are shortages dealt with?
13. What is the form of notification of receipt?
14. What is the time lag between goods arriving on the premises and the same goods being placed on the correct racks or bins?
15. What is the time lag between goods arriving and being entered on stock records?
16. How do you establish if there is a pilferage problem?
17. How would such a problem be coped with?
18. How often are the goods checked by physical count?
19. How are the goods counted and who is responsible?
20. What is the number of discrepancies between what is actually there and what is supposed to be there?
21. How are discrepancies dealt with?
22. Are any stock records kept at retail outlets or point of issue?
23. In what form? How are they posted? How are they used?

STOCK CONTROL SYSTEMS AND RECORDS

24 How do warehouses obtain replenishment supplies?
25 How are reorder quantities decided?
26 How are they adjusted if lower prices are offered for larger orders?
27 How are lead times calculated?
28 How are they used within the system?
29 How do you estimate usage rates, that is, future requirements?
30 How do you know how long existing supplies will last?
31 Do you use moving averages? Exponential smoothing? Trend corrections? Seasonal corrections?
32 How is a reorder triggered off? At branch level? At warehouse level?
33 Is there a reorder point?
34 How is it fixed?
35 How are safety stocks calculated?
36 How is frequency of deliveries determined?
37 What check is there that all stock movements are recorded?
38 Is there unnecessary duplication of data recorded?
39 Is anyone concerned handicapped by lack of information?
40 Are people in stock control informed of developments?
41 Are they properly trained? Are their skills developed to improve their capabilities and extend their responsibilities?
42 Could the stock control function continue to function if the man in charge were run over by a bus tomorrow?
43 If a computer is used for stock control:
   (a) Can you tell how its introduction has affected stock levels and service levels?
   (b) Can it be justified economically? In increased efficiency? In increased productivity?
   (c) Are future developments being considered to cope with future changes in the company's operations?

Afterword

Readers will find the British Standard on stock control a very useful adjunct to this book:

BS 5729: Parts 1-5 : 1981 Guide to stock control

Part 1 Introduction to management of stock control
Part 2 Demand assessment
Part 3 Replenishment of stock
Part 4 Data processing
Part 5 Storekeeping.

Index

ABS Computers 57
   ABS mini-computer system 55
'Apple' mini-computer 54

Barnet Health Authority supplies
system 24, 79, 82-5
   automatic recalculation of formulae 83-4
   performance assessment 84
   stock control 82-3
   stores system 82
   supplementary features 84-5
Basic control techniques 19-31
   ABC approach 19-20, 21, 30, 71
   analysis by computer 21, 22-3
   colour codes for usage classes 20-1
   controlling stock levels 21, 24-8
      measuring effectiveness 24, 28
      service level 26-7, 28
      stock-holding 28, 29
      two-bin system 21, 24, 25
   ruled-bin system 28, 30
   statistical stocktaking 30-1

Cave, C W
   rotary index file cards 42
Colt International 92-7
   physical arrangement 92
   stock control 94-7

    benefits 97
    computerisation 95
    material requisition 96
    operating routines 94-5
    organisation 94
    production programme 96
    reorder quantities 96-7
    stock master 96
    stockholding 94
Computers 53
  application to stock control 59-61
    competitive tendering 61
    establishing objectives 59
    factors for consideration 60-1
    investment decision 59
    study group approach 60
  assessing computer market 61-3
    checking with existing clients 63
    criteria 62
    maintenance and 'back-up' 62-3
  case studies on introduction into companies 65-8
    production stores study 67-8
    retailing study 65-7
  elements of systems 68-71
    central processor 70-1
    'hardware' 68
    information storage 70
    input capacity 69
    magnetic disk 57, 70
    printing out 70
    programs or 'software' 69, 71
    visual display units (VDUs) 55, 57, 69, 70
  history 53-9
    advent of mini-computer 57
    large v small 56-7
    micro/mini – differences 58-9
    three generations of 55-6
    trends for future 57-8
  introduction into company (implementation) 63-5
    'parallel running' period 64

INDEX

    staff training 64
  languages
    Cobol 56
    Fortran 56
  questions of separation or integration of functions 65

Eighty-twenty (80-20) law, *see* Basis control techniques, *ABC* approach
Electrostatic copiers 38

Filing systems 38-52
  hand-operated sorting systems 42, 50-2
  index cards 38
  microfilming 52
  rotary card files 38-9, 41, 42
  strip index 38, 39, 40
  visible-edge index 40-1, 43-50
    visible-edge form trays 41, 50
Findex system
  card sorter 51
Ford Motor Company 5
  effect of strikes 111
  production and stock control 16
    ABC approach 19, 20
    cumulative records 104
    establishing controls 101-3
    floats 103
    future development 113
    inventory 98
    parts control 104, 109
    ruled-bin system 28, 30
    schedule control 104, 105-9
    scheduling 100-1
    setting objectives 98-100
    vehicle scheduling 104, 109-12
Form design 33-8
  HMSO guide sheets 34, 35
  layout 36
  paper sizes 36-7
  spacing of entries
  weight, colour and surface finish of paper 37-8

STOCK CONTROL SYSTEMS AND RECORDS

Greater London Council Supplies Department stock control 76-9, 80-1
    monitoring reports 79, 80-1
    performance measures 76-7
    system 77-8

Hand-operated sorting systems, *see* Filing systems
Her Majesty's Stationery Office (HMSO)
    guide sheets for forms 34, 35

International Business Machines (IBM) 88
    IBM 1401 computer 56
    programming at Ward's 88

Job Specification, *see* Stock control function, organisation of

Kalamazoo
    strip index cards 40
    visible-index cards, 40, 43-7
Kardex
    stock balance record card 48
    visible-index card 48

Manufacturers' stock control 87-122
    Colt International 92-7
    Ford Motor Co. Ltd 97-113
    Pfizer Ltd 113-22
    Ward, H W, and Co. 87-92, 93
Marks and Spencer 85-6
    'pipeline' of standard merchandise 86
    stock or budgetary control 85-6
    turnover, 1980 85
Medoc Computers Limited 68
Microfilming, *see* Filing systems
Morris, William (Lord Nuffield) 5

Pareto analysis, *see* Basic control techniques, *ABC* approach
Pfizer Ltd
    products 113, 117
    size and situation 113
    stock control 113-22

INDEX

   coding system 114-15
   dead stock – and new stock 119-22
   economic order quantity 117
   manuals 115-16
   small order system 117-19
   staff 113
   stocktaking 116-17
   two-bin system 122

Rank Xerox electrostatic copiers 38
Roneo
   visible-index record card 49

Service industries stock control 75-6
   aims 75-6
   Barnet Health Authority 79, 82-5
   GLC Supplies Department 76-9, 80-1
   Marks and Spencer 85-6
Stock control function, organisation of 11-18, 53-71
   job specification 16-18
   materials management 12-16
      organising 14-16
      scope 13-14
   production and stock control 16
   relation with other functions 11-12
   use of computers 53-71
Stock control principles 3-10
   customer satisfaction 8-9
   definition of stock control 3
   management reports 10
   need for system 4-5
   objectives 5-7
   responsiveness to change 9-10
   right approach 5
Stock records design 33-52
   filing systems 38-52
   forms 33-8
Sweden
   materials administration in 12

United States of America
   development of materials management 12

Ward, H W, and Co. 87-92, 93
   computer stock control system 88-92, 93
      coding 91-2
      organisation 88-90
      reordering 90-1, 93
   introduction of computer system 87
   size and situation 87